RABBI SHLOMO GOREN

TORAH SAGE AND GENERAL

Modern Jewish Lives
volume 1

RABBI SHLOMO GOREN

TORAH SAGE AND GENERAL

by
SHALOM FREEDMAN

URIM PUBLICATIONS
Jerusalem • New York

Rabbi Shlomo Goren: Torah Sage and General
by Shalom Freedman
Series: Modern Jewish Lives – Volume 1
Series Editor: Tzvi Mauer

Copyright © 2006 by Shalom Freedman
Printed at Hemed Press in Israel.
First Edition
ISBN 965-7108-81-0

Urim Publications, P.O. Box 52287, Jerusalem 91521 Israel

Lambda Publishers Inc.
3709 13th Avenue Brooklyn, New York 11218 U.S.A.
Tel: 718-972-5449 Fax: 718-972-6307
E-mail: mh@ejudaica.com

www.UrimPublications.com

Contents

THOUGHT AND CHARACTER – Political and Religious

HAR HABAYIT: THE TEMPLE MOUNT

THE DIASPORA AND THE SHOAH

ETHICAL TEACHINGS

FAMILY AND FRIENDS

CHARACTER AND REPUTATION

AS *POSEK*

WRITINGS

IN RETROSPECT: AFTERWORD

PREFACE AND ACKNOWLEDGEMENTS

I would like to thank Rabbanit Tzvia Goren. I met with Rabbanit Goren a number of times, and she not only answered all my questions with simple straightforwardness, but made a great effort to help put me in contact with many acquaintances of Rabbi Goren. I did not, however, reach all of them. I think my characteristic deliberateness was disappointing to those accustomed to the energy and enthusiasm of Rabbi Goren, who was always *zariz le'mitzva*.

I also met with Rabbi Goren's daughters, and I felt their love and devotion to their father throughout the meeting. Rabbi Goren's son Avraham (Rami) Goren was like his mother and sisters – generous and frank – and in one long conversation in his office he told me much about the very special kind of father Rabbi Goren was.

Two of the people closest to Rabbi Goren – his faithful assistant and successor at Kommemiyut Avraham, Rabbi Dr. Yitzhak Alfassi, and Rabbi Goren's longtime army assistant and colleague, Rabbi and former Knesset Member Menachem HaCohen, also gave me valuable insights into Rabbi Goren's life and character.

I spoke with many others, attended memorial gatherings for Rabbi Goren a number of times in which those army companions who had been closest to him recalled him with affection. Over a five-year period, I spoke to tens of people in Israel who had some connection with Rabbi Goren. I did this to gauge his total effect on the Israeli public.

Aside from the interviews I conducted, I read a great part of Rabbi Goren's work and every piece of material I could find on his life and work. Unfortunately, and to my surprise and dismay, the written material on Rabbi Goren's life and work is not very great. There is no single book-length study, and not even a monograph on his life. The most extended sources are: Israel Epstein's chapter on Rabbi Goren in his book, *Heroes of Israeli Culture*; Menachem Michelson's highly informative chapter in the Israeli Army Encyclopedia on the history of the Chief Rabbinate; and two articles in the Yizkor Volume edited by Yitzhak Alfassi, one by Alfassi himself and the other by Rabbi Goren's brother-in-law, Rabbi Shear Yashuv Cohen.

A key person in enabling me to write this book, and of special help, was the veteran Israeli journalist and close Goren family friend, Shlomo Nakdimon. He not only spoke to me at length about Rabbi Goren, he went through the special trouble of searching the archives of *Yediot Ahronot* and providing valuable articles to me. A special thanks goes to my good friend, historian, and photographer, Dr. Joel Fishman, for providing photos from his archive. My good friend, Yaakov Fogelman, whose *parsha* sheet has for so many years brought learning and human interest to so many Shabbat homes, provided important contact information. Rabbi Joseph Klausner shared with me a bit of his immense learning and special expertise on the Religious Zionist world. I would also like to thank Yocheved Krems for her able copy editing of the work.

Tzvi Mauer, as the publisher, had the original idea of doing this work and provided research support throughout. My wife, Rifkah Goldberg, contributed invaluable editing help and moral support.

What I have produced is a small introductory work. A true biography of Rabbi Goren would have to tell the story of sixty years in the life of the *yishuv* and the State of Israel. It would have to touch upon most of the major events of that time, in which Rabbi Goren played a great part. A complete biographer would, also, have to be an accomplished Judaica scholar, a learned Torah person to the degree that I am not. Only such a person could really enter and comprehend the depth and range of Rabbi Goren's scholarship, and comprehensively tell the story of his life.

If I have agreed to write and publish this work, it is not because I believe it is the kind of book Rabbi Goren deserves. Rather, this work is written out of the sense that a major figure in the history of the Jewish people has not been given his due. In this sense, my task is to try to draw the main lines of his life and work. This has been done in the hope of inspiring more serious research in the future.

ADDITIONAL NOTES ON THE SOURCES
OF THE RESPECTIVE CHAPTERS

The chapters on Rabbi Goren's childhood and early life owe much to the account given by Israel Ehrlich.

The chapters on the early years of the Chief Rabbinate, the siege of Jerusalem, the preparation for the takeover of the holy places, the account of the action of the Six Day War, and the Sinai Campaign are based in good part on Menachem Michelson's account in the Israeli Army Encyclopedia.

The chapters on Rabbi Goren's trip to Poland and the Shoah are largely based on the articles of Shlomo Nakdimon in *Yediot Ahronot* as well as on Rabbi Goren's own writings on the subject.

The chapters in the Second Part of the work, stating Rabbi Goren's views, are based on his own writings, both in the Hebrew-language books and especially in the English language articles that appeared in the *Jerusalem Post*.

The chapter on Rabbi Goren's writings owes much to Rabbi Shear Yashuv Cohen's essay *"Gaon HaTorah Ha'am veHa'aretz"* from *HaMa'alot LeShlomo* (pp. 20–45).

INTRODUCTION

Rabbi Brigadier General Shlomo Goren made a unique and unforgettable contribution to the Jewish people. More than any other person, he personally embodied the ancient ideal of being both a great Jewish scholar and a remarkable soldier in the service of God and the Jewish people. He was both the first Chief Rabbi of the Israeli Army, and the most significant formative force in creating the army as a Jewish one. His great genius in learning is reflected not only in his pioneering work in Jewish law, his monumental scholarship on *Talmud Yerushalmi*, but in a wide variety of books touching upon almost all areas of modern Jewish life and thought. As a soldier for Israel, he was involved in every possible kind of duty. It began with the childhood smuggling of arms for the Haganah, and continued in his serving as a sniper in the War of Independence. It later involved the holy and dangerous task of retrieving bodies from the field of battle behind enemy lines. Still later there were the moments of glory as an inspirational presence in notable battles, most memorably in the conquest of the Old City, the Kotel, and the Temple Mount in the 1967 War.

The present work is a brief introduction to his life and teaching. It comprises a series of short chapters on the major themes of his life and thought. It is neither a chronological narrative of his life story, nor the kind of comprehensive biography that should be written about a person of Rabbi Goren's stature.

Rabbi Goren was a young *ilui* (genius in Talmudic study) whose first major work was published at seventeen. In the subsequent sixty years he wrote on a great variety of subjects. To write authoritatively on such a voluminous work is well beyond my capacity. The best that can be given by this present work is to briefly outline and hint at the character and quality of his vast literary output.

My hope is that this book will relate some of the central moments and teachings of Rabbi Goren's work, and provide a brief introduction to his life and thought. Hopefully it will give momentum to further research and interest in the life of one who both taught and embodied in his life the ideal of the Jewish struggle for, return to, and redemption of, the Land of Israel.

LIFE OF RABBI GOREN

Chapter 1

CHILDHOOD

As with most of the great pioneering figures that established both the material and spiritual foundations of the modern State of Israel, Rabbi Shlomo Goren was born in the Diaspora, outside of Israel. Shlomo Gorontschik was born on 21 *Shevat* 5768 (February 3, 1918) in the Polish village of Zambrow.* This town of 4,000 Jews was on the road between Lomza and Warsaw. Young Shlomo began his learning at home with his father, who was his teacher of Torah for many years. In early childhood the family moved to Warsaw, where he began his formal Torah learning.

His father, Rabbi Avraham Gorontschik, was a Gerrer hassid who owned two small factories in Warsaw, one for making stockings, and the other for soap production. His mother, Chaya Zippora bat Reb Eliezer Nachum Zweig, was a woman of great determination and strength, who recognized from his early childhood her son's special abilities. She called him her *ilui*, for his capacity to remember and repeat everything he had been taught, or had simply overheard.

Both parents were firm believers in the ideal of Jewish return to and building of the Land of Israel. His father was connected with *hassidei Gur* and his mother with a smaller group, the Yablona hassidim. It was with this group that the family decided to leave behind their relatively comfortable life, and set out to the then largely desolate "Palestina." They

---

* Although he changed his last name to Goren only after assuming his role as Chief Army Rabbi, we will refer to him, as well as his family members, by his later adopted Hebraisized name, Goren.

sold the factories and with the proceeds bought land in the Jezreel Valley from Keren HaKayemet, in a settlement that would later be known as Kfar Hasidim.

The conditions they encountered would have defeated far more experienced farmers. The great heat, the not especially friendly Arab neighbors, and above all, the malarial swamps made their life extremely difficult. In the land of their fathers, the Gorens were to know hunger for bread for the first time.

Shlomo, who was six when his parents left Poland, was given chores and responsibilities far beyond his age. He worked long hours in the field and often walked alone great distances to neighbors in order to bring back bread to his parents' table. He worked as a herdsman and came to feel a deep love for being alone in the natural world. Though not the physically strongest of the children in their settlement, he was the one who organized and planned defensive actions against marauding Bedouin.

Where he seemed to have trouble was in his classroom behavior. He was often sent out of the village school, something he would remark upon with both humor and regret years later. It was not that there was any maliciousness in his behavior. He was simply an extraordinarily bright and energetic child, easily bored with school lessons.

At a certain point, his father was appointed director of the swamp-clearing work in one area of the Jezreel Valley. Avraham Goren dedicated himself to the task totally, but the family paid a price for this. Malaria so frequently plagued the family that they had their own "family bed" in the hospital in Haifa. This led to their reluctantly leaving Kfar Hasidim and moving to Jerusalem.

The family had a tempting offer to return to Poland. Avraham Goren received a friend's letter suggesting that he join a new factory there as a manager. Upon hearing this offer, Zippora Goren, in words somehow echoing the Biblical Ruth, said that she would remain in the Land of Israel for the rest of her life, and be buried there. It is said that while Avraham Goren was a strong Zionist, it was the mother of the family whose passion for the Land of Israel burned most fiercely. What is apparent above all, however, is that young Shlomo had the example of two dedicated, idealistic parents willing to make great material sacrifice to make their dream of return to the land of their ancestors a reality.

Rabbi Goren's parents also had strong convictions when it came to the ideal of learning Torah. When the family moved to Jerusalem, the first thing Zippora Goren did was seek out a teacher for her son. The family arrived in Mea Shearim, and immediately went to seek out a Torah teacher, even before going to pray at the Kotel. The teacher soon took to the young Goren, convinced that he had an unusual prodigy on his hands.

The family's first stay in Jerusalem was followed by a period of time in Rechovot, where Avraham Goren was a watchman in an orchard. He would spend part of the day there and then he would learn through the evening with his son. But this somewhat idyllic Rechovot period was interrupted by the Arab riots of 1929. At this time young Shlomo began to work as a courier for the Haganah, secretly bringing weapons from one Haganah position to another.

During these riots of 1929, the Jewish community of Hebron was destroyed. Soon afterwards, the survivors of what had been the highly regarded Hebron Yeshiva opened up the yeshiva in Jerusalem.

By this time, word of young Shlomo Goren's brilliance had spread in the not-so-large learning community of Jerusalem. Certain members of the Hebron Yeshiva, hearing of his brilliance, suggested that he might try to enter the yeshiva. But when father and son Goren came to Jerusalem to request admission, they were first greeted with skepticism. The yeshiva was comprised of those who, at the youngest, were in their twenties and had learned for many years. But Avraham Goren knew his son's capabilities, and asked the *rosh yeshiva*, Rav Moshe Mordechai Epstein, to test him. The result was that Shlomo Goren became, at the age of twelve, by far the youngest person to ever study in the Hebron Yeshiva.

Rabbi Goren's childhood was a time filled with challenge and interest. He was blessed with loving, devoted idealistic parents who recognized his special gifts. From an early age, he contributed to the overall economy and well-being of the family. He also learned from his parents both a stubborness in overcoming adversity, and an ability to stick to one's goals. He was energetic and responsible beyond his years. The years to come would be ones that would test whether the great promise of his childhood was to be justified.

Chapter 2

YOUNG LEARNER

The Hebron Yeshiva, which was one of the elite learning institutions of pre-state *Eretz Yisrael*, had come to Hebron from Slobodka in Lithuania. After the Hebron massacre in 1929, which destroyed the Jewish community and in which many of the students of the yeshiva were murdered, the yeshiva moved to Jerusalem, where it began to rebuild. Here under the tutelage of HaRav Moshe Mordechai Epstein and HaRav Yechezkel Sarna, young Shlomo began a critical stage in his life of learning. Every day from the family home in Kiryat Moshe, he would make his way to the yeshiva, where he was soon recognized as an *ilui* by his peers, among whom were later to be distinguished rabbis themselves.

There is a story that the young Shlomo was learning *Gemara* one day and rapidly turning the large folio pages. When he had to leave the room, some of his fellow learners joked to each other about him, assuming that he was faking his learning to make an impression. Upon his return, hearing them laughing, Shlomo asked them what they were laughing about. When they told him, he simply told them to turn back to the page where he had begun learning. He then asked them to read out the first line of each *Tosefot* commentary on the side of the *Gemara,* at which point he picked it up and completed it by heart. He did this for all the pages, and so wiped the grin off the faces of his fellow students. He revealed to them that their fellow student was not just another bright young man, but one with truly extraordinary abilities. As would become clear throughout his learning life, he was gifted by God with an ability to not merely rapidly go through, but also understand in depth, huge quantities of material. He was gifted with a mind that comes at best to one or two in a generation.

Rabbi Yitzhak Alfassi, the prominent writer on hassidism who was Rav Goren's assistant for many years at the Kommemiyut Avraham Synagogue, which Rabbi Goren founded in the name of his father, reported a remarkable incident that occurred at one of Rabbi Goren's frequent visits to a Gerrer *simcha*. There he was greeted by a whole host of giants of learning who began to discuss a certain *sugya* or Talmudic problem. Rabbi Goren first stated the problem and his own position, and then, one by one imitating the voices of each of the prospective speakers, said exactly what they wanted to say about the problem. He encompassed in his learning the understanding that others had or would develop of the problem, and took into account their positions in formulating his own. This would no doubt be one of the important qualities that would be involved in his becoming a *posek* (a halachic authority) of great importance.

His remarkable mind was also the first quality that moved two of the giants of the generation, Rabbi Isser Zalman Meltzer and Rabbi Avraham Yitzhak HaKohen Kook to, in effect, become his partners in learning and his teachers. The two great masters were moved not only the genius of the young Goren, but also by another formidable quality of his – his tremendous energy and enthusiasm in learning. This energy was concentrated very early in the production of Rabbi Goren's first work of scholarship. At the tender age of seventeen, he produced his work *Nezer HaKodesh*, on the Rambam's halachic rulings regarding those offerings disqualified for Temple sacrifice. Both Rav Kook and Rav Meltzer wrote lavish *haskamot* praising the work, heralding the coming of a new Talmudic genius.

In those early years there had been a remarkable transformation from the restless youth the walls of the school could not contain, to the serious Talmudic student able to *matmid* – sit and persevere in learning for long hours. The habit of sitting and learning for hours that he developed at the Hebron Yeshiva, which came to be despite the tremendous worldly obligations he would later take on, would be with him through his entire adult life. Students of his in later years were amazed at his always being the first to appear at the yeshiva in the morning and the last one to leave at the end of the day. Throughout his life, according to Rabbi Alfassi, he spent much time learning by himself. In his youth, there was a small shack in the Kiryat Moshe district where the young Goren would sit for hours and learn by himself. Even later in life when he would be involved in numerous areas of action requiring the greatest part of his attention and time, Rabbi Goren would always find time for learning. Years later, his day with his staff in the Chief Rabbinate's office would always begin with an hour of *Gemara* learning.

His extraordinary capacity for and dedication to learning does not, however, explain how he had the confidence and boldness to produce a significant work of scholarship at the age of seventeen. This work appeared on 24 *MarCheshvan*, the same date on which sixty years later Rabbi Goren left the world. The spiritual birth initiated by this publication would be the start of a career in writing and scholarship that would continue throughout his life. Through these years, Rabbi Goren produced a monumental work of scholarship in most fields of Torah learning: in Halacha, in *Aggada*, in the *parshat hashavua*, in the Revealed, and the Hidden Torah. The most practical and significant application of this learning was in Rabbi Goren's making halachic rulings. Rabbi Goren became a pioneering and often highly controversial figure in his role as *posek*. In the remarkable breadth of his scholarship, Rabbi Goren bears greatest resemblance to the Torah figure of his own time, who, arguably, made the most significant impression upon him, the first Chief Rabbi of Israel, Rabbi Avraham Yitzhak HaKohen Kook, *ztz"l*.

Chapter 3

RABBI AVRAHAM YITZHAK HAKOHEN KOOK *ztz"l*

There is no doubt that one of the most important influences on the life and especially the worldview of young Shlomo Goren, was the then-Chief Rabbi of Palestine, one of the great thinkers and teachers of modern Jewish history, Rabbi Avraham Yitzhak HaKohen Kook. It is not clear when the young *ilui* first met the great man. There are stories to the effect that in the Jerusalem of Mandate days, Avraham Goren would, like the father of Mozart, take his young genius into various households where he would have him demonstrate his precocious abilities. It may have been on one such expedition that young Shlomo first encountered Rav Kook. But Rabbanit Goren tells of another venue, a certain holiday place near Haifa where Rav Kook would spend the summer months. Here the young Shlomo, with his characteristic daring, would approach Rav Kook and speak with him on matters of Torah. After a time Rav Kook took to delighting in the young *ilui*'s presence and so frequently invited him to be a guest at the Kook home in Jerusalem.

Israel Ehrlich, in his excellent biographical chapter on Rabbi Goren in *People and Events in the History of Israel* (Tel Aviv: Morasha, 1995) suggests that it was meetings with Rav Kook that were of essential importance in forming Rabbi Goren's religious Zionist view of the world. Ehrlich says that when Rabbi Goren was studying in the Hebron Yeshiva, he was a frequent guest at the home of Rav Kook. Ehrlich states that in a short time Rav Kook recognized the potential greatness of young Shlomo. They would engage in long and fervent discussions, and Rabbi Goren learned much from Rav Kook about the love of *Eretz Yisrael* and there he acquired an interest in practical halacha.

It was at Rav Kook's home that Rabbi Goren also met someone who would be an important friend in the future, Rav Kook's only son and spiritual heir, Rav Zvi Yehuda. He also met there the man who was to become his father-in-law, the great interpreter of Rav Kook's writing, the *nazir*, Rabbi David Cohen.

The subsequent path of Rabbi Goren's life confirmed the centrality of this early connection with the life and thought of Rav Kook. Rabbi Goren lived a life dedicated to the ideals that Rav Kook taught in regard to the sanctity of the people and the Land of Israel. Rabbi Goren also learned from Rav Kook his exceptional openness to secular Jews, and a deep and abiding sense of the value of Jewish unity. Both men shared an openness and understanding of the special situation of Jews trying to build a land and a state after two thousand years of exile.

For this understanding of non-religious Jews building the Land of Israel, both Rav Kook and Rabbi Goren were attacked by more narrow-minded religious leaders. Yet both courageously persisted in this approach of concern for the well-being of the people of Israel, *Klal Yisrael*, and not only for those who shared their own special worldview.

There was much more in common between them. Both were Torah giants whose creative gifts extended into a variety of areas of traditional Jewish scholarship. Both men were thinkers centered on the idea of Jewish history as a redemptive process. Both are noted for extraordinary deeds of personal charity and sacrifice for the people.

The special esteem and affection Rav Kook had for young Shlomo is reflected in the warm words of recommendation that preface Rabbi Goren's first published volume. The gratitude and esteem of Rabbi Goren for Rav Kook was to be nobly exemplified in an action taken by Rabbi Goren forty years after the day of Rav Kook's death. On that day Shlomo Goren was elected Chief Rabbi of Israel. The first thing the new Chief Rabbi did was to ascend to the Mount of Olives (*Har HaZaytim*) and pray there at the gravesite of the one who had been his greatest spiritual mentor.

Chapter 4

UNIVERSITY STUDENT

In 1935, at the age of eighteen, Shlomo Goren enrolled at the Hebrew University at Mt. Scopus (*Har HaTzofim*) that had been opened just ten years before. There he studied Mathematics, Classics, and Greek. He was, by all accounts, a brilliant student and the knowledge he gained at the university would serve him in good stead much later in his life, both in his role as *posek* (halachic authority) and in future teaching work. Many years later, he employed the background in philosophy he acquired at the university in his teaching of Jewish Philosophy at Haifa University. In time, Rabbi Goren became known for his remarkable combination of being both soldier and scholar, and he also became known for his capacity for mastering both Torah and secular learning. This capacity would aid him in many ways; for instance it was a crucial element in his relationship with David Ben-Gurion, with whom he frequently discussed religious philosophy.

During his years as a university student, Rabbi Goren also continued in his Torah learning. His tremendous energy, which enabled him to take on many more responsibilities than the ordinary person, was also evident in these years.

The university also helped him in another inadvertent, but most important, way. Tzvia Cohen, the woman who was to become his wife and mother of his children and the constant source of strength and stability in his life, studied at the university at the same time. Her great intelligence and wise judgment were to serve him well in the turbulent years ahead.

Chapter 5

COURAGEOUS YOUNG SOLDIER

At a very young age, Shlomo Goren actively participated in the defense of his community at Kfar Hasidim. In 1936, at the outbreak of Arab rioting, he heeded the call of the hour and joined the Jewish defense forces then organizing in the *yishuv*, the early, modern Israeli settlement. Through the years, he did military duty as an auxiliary special policeman (*notar*). For a time, he was also a member of the Jewish underground group Lehi.

In 1947, at a time when the *yishuv* was already fighting for its life, Rabbi Goren understood that he could not avoid the call and continue to give all his effort to learning alone. He knew that he had to be a part of the battle for the defense of the *yishuv*. He joined the Haganah, and in a short while was considered one of the expert marksmen in Jerusalem. He was later given training on a heavy machine gun. Wherever he was, two qualities of his became immediately apparent: his capacity for leadership and responsibility – for making vital decisions – and his own great personal courage. Rabbi Goren was one of those rare people who seemed to know no fear for his own personal safety. In fact, his life is studded with heroic acts in which he volunteered to do – at great personal risk – what others were reluctant to do. During and after the Israeli War of Independence, and in fact through a period of close to twenty-five years, he risked his life to recover the bones of soldiers for proper burial. During the Six Day War, he marched out ahead of a company of soldiers racing to the Old City. Time and time again, in military operations, he acted as if no enemy bullet could touch him. Perhaps he had in mind the religious teaching that one who goes on a mission of *mitzva* can know no great harm. But the fact is that with extraordinary courage he had extraordinary achievements. He took risks to get important jobs done. This is no doubt one source of the great admiration many of the military people of secular background had for him. He got the job done no matter what the risk.

Asked whether he feared anything, Rabbi Goren said that as a child he had feared dogs. But his daughter reports that in later years, during his morning swim at the Herzliya beach, he would chase off packs of wild dogs with a stick. Apparently, that fear, too, had been overcome in time.

Time and time again he put himself at great risk in the service of the Jewish defense forces without hesitation. Whether in the War of Independence, the Sinai Campaign, the Six Day War, the War of Attrition, or the Yom Kippur War, Rabbi Goren always went to the front line, where he would bring strength and inspiration to others.

He was even impervious to the danger when shells fell close to him. He was fearless and determined.

One reason for this was his absolute conviction of the rightness of Jewish acts of self-defense. His courage was not an individual caprice, an act of bravado and individual defiance, a modern existential hero's playing with fate. Instead, it was born out of his belief in the rightness of the struggle he was engaged in, and his sense that he was doing God's work. He believed himself part of a people being reborn in their ancient homeland, fulfilling the Divine promise, the covenant of God with Israel. His actions were not dictated by some narcissistic sense of striving for personal glory, but rather out of what must be done to serve and help the people.

His closest associate for many years, the man who went with him through the battles of the Six Day War, Rabbi Menachem HaCohen, pointed out how tireless Rabbi Goren was in serving the soldiers, in doing everything possible to meet their religious needs in time of battle. Rabbi Goren did not think of his own personal comfort and ease, but rather, he

Rabbi Shlomo Goren at the beginning of his service as a military chaplain,
March 1, 1949. GPO, photographer Hans Pinn.

pushed himself relentlessly to be on the battlelines where he felt his presence was most needed. He also made great efforts to understand what soldiers were going through. This is no doubt one reason he went through paratrooper training at a relatively advanced age.

The highlight of Rabbi Goren's activities as a soldier came in that heroic rush in June 1967 to the Old City of Jerusalem, to the Temple Mount and the Western Wall. In that decisive battle, the weapons he held in his hand were a sefer Torah and a *shofar*. His standup charge toward the gate, while drawing enemy fire, would seem to some foolhardy and reckless. But to many soldiers it was the inspirational action of a leader going at the head of their troops into battle, as Israeli officers are required to do.

Chapter 6

RELATIONSHIP WITH BEN-GURION

In the first stages of the War of Independence, the reputation of the courageous fighter who was also a *gadol* in Torah reached those in high places. Both the then-chief Ashkenazi rabbi of Israel, Rabbi Israel HaLevi Herzog, and the Rishon le'Zion, Rav Uziel, when hearing that Ben-Gurion was looking for someone to begin to head up the religious services division of the incipient Israeli Army, thought of Shlomo Goren. They called upon him to take on this duty. At first, he refused on the grounds that there was nothing more vital than dedicating himself wholly to fighting for the defense of the *yishuv*. It would have been immoral in his eyes to abandon his men and unit at a time fighting was in full force. Moreover, he was very much concerned that any army chaplaincy would be formed as a kind of ghetto within the army, i.e., for religious soldiers only.

All his life, Shlomo Goren was a passionate believer in the unity of the people of Israel, *Am Yisrael*. He did not believe that it was morally right, for instance, for non-religious soldiers to be the *Shabbos goyim* for the religious. He did not believe religious soldiers should use their religiousness as a means of privilege, or escaping their duty. Just the opposite, he believed their religiousness should lead them to be even more conscienscious in serving *Am Yisrael*. So he would not agree to head up the proposed "Religious Services Unit" unless he had an understanding that his authority would be in effect throughout the army, for both religious and non-religious soldiers. There could not be a kosher kitchen for one smaller set of soldiers, and a larger non-kosher kitchen for those who had no such concerns. *Kashrut* supervision, Rabbi Goren insisted, would have to be instituted throughout the army. In the matter of religious services there would not be each group praying according to its own local custom, but rather a *nusach achid,* a single prayer style and liturgy, that would unite all.

At a lull in the fighting in early 1948, at a time when he could afford to leave his unit, Rabbi Goren agreed to become the head of the army's religious services. In doing so, he began one of the most productive personal relationships of his life, one that would be of great importance to the people of Israel. He began his relationship with Israel's great founding father and first prime minister, David Ben-Gurion. For close to twenty-five years, these two giants disagreed and quarreled vociferously with each other on questions of "state and religion." Their relations were characterized by total frankness, honesty, and mutual respect. This was in great part because of the values and purpose they shared. Ben-Gurion was by no means formally religious, and it is said that in all his years in Israel he stepped into a synagogue only one time. But Ben-Gurion and Shlomo Goren shared a sense of the historical urgency of founding a Jewish state, and of working in it for the reconstruction of the Jewish people. They shared a certain conception of power and historical responsibility. They also shared the determination to bring about a greater unity and common purpose in *Am Yisrael.* And this when both of them were deeply aware of how sharp divisions had helped bring great tragedy to *Am Israel* in the past.

They were bridges to different worlds for each other. Ben-Gurion connected Shlomo Goren with the very heart of the Zionist power structure. And Shlomo Goren connected Ben-Gurion with what then seemed to be the most dynamic and vital forces within the religious community. Another common element in their mutual respect had to do with their respective characters. Both of them were not simply strong-willed. They were both strong and decisive in action. And they were both fighters, with enormous stores of determination who, once they set out on a course, were not moved from it.

Rabbi Goren being congratulated by Ben-Gurion and Moshe Dayan at his
installation as Chief Ashkenazi Rabbi of Tel Aviv, June 15, 1971.
GPO, photographer Fritz Cohen.

Rabbi Goren with Chief Rabbi Yehuda Unterman and Rabbi Elyashiv (center)
during the Chief Rabbinate elections at Heichal Shlomo, Jerusalem, Mar. 17, 1964.
GPO, photographer Fritz Cohen.

In one of the great historically decisive moments of the Jewish people, Ben-Gurion overrode his own ministers, defied the Secretary of State of the United States, and – against long odds – declared and led the successful struggle for the establishment of the State of Israel. Rabbi Goren in numerous instances of his life – perhaps none so great and dramatic as that of Ben-Gurion – showed the same willingness to fight for what he saw as right, against all odds and authority, only to win the day in the end. One telling example of this came years later when he resisted all orders, and went in to open up the Cave of the Patriarchs (Machpelah Cave) in Hebron once again for Jewish prayer.

In the early years of the army, Rabbi Goren established, with Ben-Gurion's support, kosher kitchens throughout the army. He began programs for educating the soldiers in the meaning of the holidays. He, too, began his unprecedented and remarkable activity as *posek* for the Israeli Army. In other words, he began to take those actions that made it possible for completely religious soldiers to serve in the army, and enabled the non-religious soldiers to have a deeper knowledge and understanding of their own tradition.

He began what were for him perhaps the most productive and happy years of his life – and this too because he was, in his own eyes and mind, a soldier as well. And in establishing religious services for the army he did this not simply in a formal and external way, but with deepest concern for and understanding of the needs of the individual soldier.

Chapter 7

First Passover Seder

From 1948 to 1972, Shlomo Goren was Chief Rabbi of the Israeli Army.

He came to this position at first very reluctantly, and only through the constant persuading of a large number of people, including the then-Chief Rabbis, Rabbi Herzog and Rabbi Ben-Zion Uziel. A few months before Pesach in 1948, religious soldiers came to Rabbi Goren (then still Gorontschik) and requested that he prepare Pesach for them. Rabbi Goren refused, saying that he was a regular soldier like them. They went to Chief Rabbi Herzog, who called for Goren and asked him to take upon himself the whole area of religious supervision for the Israeli Army, then in the process of its formation. A few days later it was General Shaltiel, the commander of forces in Jerusalem, who came to Goren and told him that all of the many religious soldiers were complaining about the absence of services to meet their special needs. At first, Rabbi Goren conditioned his agreement on his being able to continue his military duties at night. He was also planning a great work, a new edition of the *Jerusalem Talmud*. Rabbi Goren also told Shaltiel that he did not wish to be an army rabbi; that he entered as a fighter and wished to remain as one. Shaltiel told him that he was truly useful as a fighter, but that Rabbi Herzog had told him there was no man more suitable in Israel to be the head of such a religious service than Goren. Goren began his army rabbinical service with the idea that it would be temporary. He had no idea that it would become a major part of his life's work, extending for twenty-four years.

Rabbi Goren began to work as military rabbi in February 1948. His first undertaking was kashering the kitchen of Jerusalem's major army camp, Schneller. To this task, he enlisted his father, who was made *kashrut* supervisor of Schneller.

That Pesach, Rav Goren also arranged for kosher Passover Seders in the greater-Jerusalem area bases. Ben-Gurion came to the one in Schneller, and when his presence was noted, hundreds of soldiers crowded around. Ben-Gurion spoke briefly, saying, "This is the first true holiday of freedom since the destruction of the Temple." The crowd was so great that Ben-Gurion was not able to walk out, and had to leave by being lifted up and carried out above the crowd.

The First Passover Haggadah

The very first Passover Haggada published by the Israeli Defense Forces (IDF) was in *Nisan* (April) 5649/1949. All subsequent Pesach *haggadot* published by the army were different and more elaborate, but since this first Haggada was published in a rush right after the 1948 War of Liberation, the army used the plates of another Haggada published in the previous year by the Lewin-Epstein Jerusalem Publishing Company. The big difference between that earlier edition and this first IDS edition is the fact that in the inner cover there's a letter addressed to the soldiers from the first Chief Rabbi of the IDF, Shlomo Gorontschik, later to become the Chief Rabbi of Israel, Shlomo Goren, and liberator of Jerusalem.

In the forward he writes in Hebrew:

> After 2,000 years of physical and spiritual slavery, we have merited to celebrate the festival of freedom...the light of redemption and freedom that has shone over the skies of Israel has shined upon us anew. And just as we left Egypt and saw miracles of God, so too we saw in the War of Independence that we waged in our land. Raise high the flag of freedom that you have acquired by your hands in great bravery and self sacrifice as we envision the complete

Redemption and celebrate the Festival of Passover in the Temple of God in Jerusalem, that shall be rebuilt!

–Shlomo Gorontschik, Chief Rabbi of the IDF

Chapter 8

Saving Jerusalem From Jordanian Invasion

There is a remarkable incident from the War of Independence reported in the "Army Encylopedia." It relates to the siege of Jerusalem. According to the encyclopedia, on May 14 the commander of the Jerusalem forces came to Rabbi Goren and told him that the Jordanians were about to invade. He said that there was no available manpower to dig trenches that could protect the city in the north from where the invaders were to come. He asked Rabbi Goren to mobilize the yeshiva students, the only available population capable of doing the work.

Rabbi Goren resisted, as this would involve causing a massive violation of the Sabbath. He said he could not do this on his own authority, and went to Chief Rabbi Herzog, who gave a *heter.* But this was not enough. He had to go as well to Rav Dushinsky of the *Eida HaHareidit,* and ask his permission. Rav Dushinsky was sympathetic, but said he himself could not give permission.

Rabbi Goren realized that the fate of the city was in his hands. So he went by himself from yeshiva to yeshiva, mobilizing students for the work. Rabbi Goren, by his great conviction, was able to convince yeshiva students that the *pikuach nefesh* involved in saving the city required doing this work on Shabbat, making it not a sin at all, but indeed a requirement. The students were pursuaded by Rabbi Goren, and worked all night digging trenches in the northern part of the city.

On the morning of the next day, the Jordanian tanks approached the city and the first tank that entered fell into one of the anti-tank trenches that had been built. When a second started to go in, the rest of the tanks turned around and went back.

The city was saved from the Jordanian forces in great part due to the initiative and determination of Rabbi Goren.

Chapter 9

ESTABLISHING THE ARMY RABBINATE

Rabbi Goren's pioneering and decisive role as first chief chaplain of the Israeli military forces was not only on the battlefield. In order to establish *kashrut* in all kitchens in *Tzahal*, in order to ensure that Shabbat would truly be a Shabbat of rest, Rabbi Goren had to engage in many struggles against those indifferent or even hostile to religious practice. Although a good percentage of the soldiers in the Jerusalem area in 1948 were observant; the great majority of those in the entire army were not. Moreover, at a time when the *yishuv* was struggling to establish itself, and there was scarcity in all things, the military chaplaincy was not, to say the least, a high priority area for government budgets.

In one noted incident in 1949, Rabbi Goren wrote a long letter to Ben-Gurion threatening to resign after not receiving promised supplies for religious services. Rabbi Goren would not be part of a show, and if the supplies would not arrive in time to enable the army kitchens to be kosher for the Pesach of that year, he would not continue serving as Chief Rabbi of the Israeli Army.

This particular crisis was averted when Ben-Gurion urgently dispatched people to the United States to find the appropriate religious supplies and send them urgently to the rabbinate. But this was not the only crisis. On another occasion, Rabbi Goren threatened to resign when his orders about keeping Shabbat were undermined by other officers. Once again, Rabbi Goren took his fight to Ben-Gurion and won the day.

Rabbi Goren was also concerned that the practice of desecrating Shabbat was increasing in the army. He was concerned about the question of appropriate cultural activity for the soldiers on Shabbat. He complained about the difficulty of printing and distributing vital and elementary educational material about the holidays. He was also disturbed that the smallest piece of educational material was required to undergo a strict military censorship, impeding its timely distribution.

It is perhaps difficult for those living in a milieu that is religious to understand exactly the great resistance Rabbi Goren had to overcome to accomplish these things. In establishing the religious services, he was swimming against the tide. He was doing something that a great percentage of the people in the army not only thought was irrelevant, but opposed outright.

But his courage, his determination, and his absolute dedication to his faith and religious principles served the people of Israel well.

In later years, Rabbi Goren was known – and was even maligned – for being a controversial figure. But what it is important to understand is that in the main controversies of his work and his life, he was struggling for matters of religious principle. And his willingness to take on those greater in power and authority were proof that his courage was not simply a physical, but a spiritual one.

It is fair to say that without his determination and will, it is doubtful that a good number of the religious soldiers who have served in the Israeli Army would have been, in all good conscience, able to do so.

Chapter 10

MITZVA OF BRINGING FALLEN SOLDIERS
TO *KEVER YISRAEL*

One of the most difficult of the tasks of the military rabbinate is bringing the fallen in war to proper burial. This task was especially difficult after the Israeli War of Independence. There were bodies scattered in a wide variety of locations, many still behind enemy lines. To extricate these bodies often involved complex political and military operations. Above all, it required a dedicated group of people willing to risk their lives, when necessary, to fulfill their duty.

Rabbi Goren's actions in fulfilling this *mitzva* are legendary. He often went into territory where no one else would go, risked his life leaping through minefields to get to locations where bodies were scattered. For his courage in this, he not only won the gratitude of many of the families who could at least give proper burial to their loved ones, he won the admiration of Israeli society as a whole.

Rabbi Goren brought to *kever Yisrael* the *lamed-heh,* the thirty-five, fallen in the convoy meant to relieve besieged Gush Etzion. In the Faluja pocket, in Latrun, and in dozens of other locations, searches were made for the bodies of the fallen. On one occasion the situation was so dangerous that Rabbi Goren signed an order giving a *get* (divorce) to his wife, should he not return, i.e., to free her for remarriage should he be declared missing. On another occasion, the Jordanians could not understand how, in pouring rain, a high-ranking officer like Rabbi Goren

Senior officers on board a navy ship with Rabbi Goren at the funeral ceremony
for Dakar sailors lost in action.
From *People and Events in Jewish History* by Israel Ehrlich.

Rabbi Goren receives the bodies of pilots who fell behind enemy lines.
From *People and Events in Jewish History* by Israel Ehrlich.

would wander out in such difficult terrain to search for those no longer alive. On yet another occasion, Rabbi Goren recovered the remains of bodies that had been mutilated by the Jordanians. In Gush Etzion, he saw the total devastation made by the Jordanians of the four settlements that had been destroyed in the war.

In this process of searching for remains over a period of two years, more than one thousand soldiers, and in some cases civilians, were brought to *kever Yisrael*. Rabbi Goren had a dedicated team of people for this work, including his major-assistant, Yitzhak Meir.

In doing this painful and difficult work, Rabbi Goren exemplified the principle of *acharai* (after me) that was so important in the early days of the Israeli Army. He was the commander who went first and took the greatest risk.

In performing this most important *mitzva*, he again showed a courage and dedication that characterized the whole of his public life.

Chapter 11

ACTIVITIES AS AN ARMY RABBI

Rabbi Goren's activities in establishing the army rabbinate were wide-ranging. He was involved in questions of principle and questions of minute detail. On one of the major issues, the question of whether to have separate religious units or to integrate all soldiers into a unified framework, he worked assiduously for the integration. He argued that it is a mistake to create "ghettos" for religious soldiers within the army. Many people opposed Rabbi Goren on this, especially those who came from the extreme left of the political spectrum and feared imposition of religious standards on their own people. In this matter, Rabbi Goren went to David Ben-Gurion and convinced him that the unity of the army and the people required integrated units. Ben-Gurion sided with him, and the army became a significant area for social integration through the years in the young Israeli society.

Guided by the principle of the unity of the people of Israel, Rabbi Goren and Rabbi Menachem HaCohen together worked to create a *nusach achid*, a siddur and a prayer service that would work for all the different ethnic communities, *eidot*, of Israel. Rabbi Goren and Menachem HaCohen also wrote special prayers for the various units of the army. Among these are the "Prayer Before Going Out to Battle," the "Prayer for Pilots," the "Prayer for Submarine Crews," and the "Memorial Service for Soldiers Fallen in the Wars of Israel." He was continually involved in establishing

Rabbi Goren visiting troops on Syrian front during the Succot holiday week, Oct. 13, 1973. GPO, photographer Herman Chanania.

Rabbi Goren sharing a kosher meal of battle rations in the field with soldiers. From *People and Events in Jewish History* by Israel Ehrlich.

and maintaining *kashrut* throughout the army. He created the means for working to provide religious education to those soldiers who wanted it. Above all, he was the *posek* on the many questions religious soldiers have in regard to conflicting obligations, maintaining their religious observance, and doing their army duty. Through his years of army service, Rabbi Goren received thousands of such questions, and his responsa have been published in four volumes under the title *Meishiv Milchama*. In this area he was the great pioneer, the first to take up the kinds of questions the homeless and landless and army-less Jewish people had had no need to ask for 2,000 years. As with so many other areas of his activity, Rabbi Goren first dared to enter where others would not yet dare to go.

Rabbi Goren always considered himself a fighting soldier, and had the greatest possible sympathy and identification with the dilemmas of the soldiers in the field. He understood the problems of the man in the field in a way that no one else of his rabbinic stature could. Moreover as a *talmid chacham,* he brought the knowledge and the system of study, which enabled him to truly tackle – halachically – each problem. His responsa are a model of thoroughness, rigor, and, at the same time, humane consideration.

Rabbi Goren also believed that an essential part of the task of the army rabbinate was in educating the soldiers in the values and teachings of Judaism. It is suitable to remember that he always began his day with a *shiur* in *Gemara* with his staff. He was continually teaching as he dealt with the countless problems and decisions he made each day. He visited base after base; was almost constantly in motion, and would go even to the most remote areas; spoke with the soldiers; learned their problems, and gave his halachic response to them. As Chief Rabbi, he established the division of the army rabbinate, which deals with identification of and burial of the fallen. He was deeply involved with the question of *agunot,* and his humane and caring consideration of the families of the fallen is perhaps, more than anything else, the sign of how deeply a compassionate human being he was.

The Chief Rabbinate of the army published the magazine

Rabbi Goren and his wife Tzvia next to Ben-Gurion and his wife Paula
at a parade marking the end of an officer's course for women, May 18, 1966.
GPO, photographer Moshe Milner.

Photo of joint IDF senior staff with Ben-Gurion and Defense Ministry officials.
Rabbi Goren is in the back row second from right, May 1, 1961. GPO.

Rabbi Goren in conversation with Torah greats Rabbi Bezalel Zolty (center)
and Rabbi Yitzhok Hutner.
From *People and Events in Jewish History* by Israel Ehrlich.

Rabbi Goren between Torah greats Rabbi Shabtai Yogel (right)
and Rabbi Aharon Kotler, at a Great Assembly opening.
From *People and Events in Jewish History* by Israel Ehrlich.

Machanayim, a good part of which was written by Rabbi Goren. The magazine discussed the problems confronting the soldiers and the state. Before each holiday, special educational material was prepared. And while it might be surmised that these materials were of most interest to religious soldiers, it is clear they had a broader aim. For Rabbi Goren, as well as for his great teacher, Rav Kook, there was no such thing as a non-religious Jew, as one who could not be moved to return to greater closeness to religious life.

In all his activities in the military rabbinate, Rabbi Goren showed boundless enthusiasm and energy. He slept only a few hours a night and he never complained of tiredness, but only pushed forward to do his duty in the best way he could. He set a remarkable example for all those who worked with him and for those who so admired him. It is said that no man is a hero to his valet, but for Rabbi Goren, precisely the opposite is the case. Those who knew him closest and were nearest to him are those who most passionately attest to his dedication and greatness in pursing the realization of tasks before him.

It is fair to say that not only was he the chief architect of the military rabbinate, but also helped it acquire its hard-earned place as one of the most respected army units. In doing this, he not only enabled observant soldiers to serve in the army, he made the army itself a Jewish institution. He did this so that the first Jewish army in 2,000 years would not be simply an army of Jews, but a Jewish army.

Chapter 12

SINAI CAMPAIGN

By the time the 1956 Sinai Campaign had begun, the military rabbinate was established as a respectable wing of the army. Instead of being considered an irritant, it had a recognized status. By the time the Sinai Campaign got underway, there were regular and *miluim* (reserve) units of the *Chevra Kadisha* (burial society) already established.

This campaign brought to the fore a number of important halachic questions. Could the army train on Shabbat? Is it permissible to bring supplies to field units on Shabbat? The shortage of bread raised the question by the chief supply officer of whether it would be possible to bake matzah for field rations on a Shabbat?

In a special meeting of the staff of the military rabbinate, Rabbi Goren was authorized to go to the Chief Rabbis of Israel with these questions. He returned with answers that enabled the army to continue to function under a halachic framework. Soldiers were granted permission to train on Shabbat.

Another problem related to the shortage of meat that had been kashered for the field units. Rabbi Goren was troubled that the whole system of *kashrut* he had worked so painstakingly to establish would be destroyed if not-yet-koshered meat was supplied to the units, as not always would these units have the water and salt required to do the kashering. So a special operation was undertaken in which the rabbinate sent a large number of special inspectors to the army meat plants to ensure the *kashrut* of all their products.

Shortly before the outbreak of the Sinai Campaign hostilities in 1956, Rabbi Goren went down to the south to help strengthen the various battlefield units. On route, in the woody area near Ketziot, he was inspired to write the "Prayer Before Going Out to Battle," which was immediately printed and reached the soldiers before they had to go into battle.

Rabbi Goren joined the forces that entered the outskirts of Gaza before the city's conquest. On the Friday night before, in the field, he held a special *Kabbalat Shabbat* prayer in which a great number of the soldiers who were to go into battle participated. Instilling the soldiers with faith and strength was his constant task.

During the time of the fighting, there was an official army decision to change the former practice of burial, in order to show greater honor to the fallen, and bury the dead temporarily near the field of battle. Later they were brought back for official burial in the military cemeteries within Israel. This was an extremely difficult task for the *Chevra Kadisha*, as each individual soldier had to be given his own separate service in which the members of the *Chevra Kadisha* were the stand-ins for the loved ones not present. This was done in complete accordance with the principle Rabbi Goren exemplified all his years in the military; the principle of sparing no personal effort in order to provide the maximum possible concern and care for the dignity of the individual.

Rabbi Goren with General Rafael Eitan at the dedication of the
Parachutist's House in Ramat Gan, May 10, 1973. GPO.

Chief Rabbi Shlomo Goren confering in the field with General Rafael Eitan,
May 11, 1982. GPO, photographer Yaacov Sa'ar.

Chapter 13

FIRST RELIGIOUS PARATROOPER

At one of his frequent visits in the field, Rabbi Goren confronted a young commander who had already made a name for himself, Ariel Sharon. Rabbi Goren insisted that the unit that Sharon commanded integrate fully with the rest of the army in terms of *kashrut*. The young commander challenged Rabbi Goren, and said that if he had one religious soldier in his paratroop unit then he would agree to have a kosher kitchen for the entire unit. Rabbi Goren immediately volunteered and went through paratroop training. And he acquired his wings, even though in one of the practice jumps he broke his leg. Nonetheless he had proven his point, and the kitchen of this unit was made kosher.

Many years later, a good percentage of the soldiers in similar units were religious. It is doubtful that this would have ever happened had not Rabbi Goren set the precedent and the standard that others could follow.

Chapter 14

Israel Prize

In 1962, Rabbi Goren was awarded the Israeli prize for his work on the *Jerusalem Talmud*. Surveying the contribution made by Rabbi Goren, Abraham Goldberg, in the *Jerusalem Post*, points out that Rabbi Goren presented an edition of the first five chapters of the first tractate. Goldberg writes that Rabbi Goren used the text of the first printed edition (Venice 1552) of the *Yerushalmi*. He interprets it in relation to parallel passages in the *Babylonian Talmud*, and commentary of *Tosefta* and various *Midrashim*. Goldberg also writes that it is both a critical commentary "close to the scientific spirit" and yet written "in the well-established rabbinic tradition."

Rabbi Goren had begun his work on the *Yerushalmi* many years before, and had been forced to interrupt it when called to serve in the army and establish the army rabbinate. The prize seemed to signal that he was on his way to fulfilling his dream of bringing out a new edition of the work popularly called "The Talmud of *Eretz Yisrael*."

Chapter 15

PLAN FOR THE HOLY PLACES

Among Rabbi Goren's more interesting works after the Sinai Campaign in 1956 was the plan he drew up for protection of the "holy places." In other words, he anticipated that at some point the Israeli Army would enter and recapture Old Jerusalem.

This plan was liberal in spirit, calling for Israel to be a generous custodian of all holy places. It called for the Israeli government to ensure the right of worship of the major faiths at their own holy places. It had a special provision forbidding fighting in the area of holy places. And it said that Israeli soldiers could fire back at those shooting at them from holy places only if there was danger to their lives. It even made a list of places so holy that firing back was not allowed there. Among these were the Temple Mount mosques.

This program ironically did help ensure that Muslims (and Christians) would be able to pray at their holy places, but did not, for reasons not under Rabbi Goren's control, ensure that also Jews would have a right to pray at their most holy place, the Temple Mount.

Chapter 16

Six Day War: Jerusalem Reunited

In 1948, when the fighting between Arabs and Jews finished, the city of Jerusalem was left divided. The Temple Mount, the Western Wall, and the Jewish Quarter were in Arab hands. After 1948, the Jews of Israel could not cross the line and visit their most holy places. They could only climb to high places and look with longing across the divided city. During this time, Jordan was interested in developing its capital in Amman, and largely neglected Jerusalem. Jewish holy sites were desecrated, including the cemetery on the Mount of Olives.

It is safe to say that the great majority of the people of Israel during this time lived with a great longing in their heart, a longing to return to their most sacred places. In 1961, a Jerusalem-born paratroop commander named Mordechai Gur had a conversation with Rabbi Goren that would later turn out to be of historic significance. He told him of his plan, should there be an outbreak of fighting, to retake the Old City of Jerusalem. And he promised Rabbi Goren that he would be able to join with his forces should this take place.

In 1967, the Egyptians closed the Straits of Tiran, a clear act of war, and forced a long period of waiting and tension upon Israel, while the United States and other forces tried to find a diplomatic solution to the problem. There was a tremendous anxiety in Israel and throughout the Jewish world at this time regarding the possible destruction of the state. It was less than twenty-five years since the Shoah (Holocaust), the murder of over one-third of the Jewish people by the Nazis and their collaborators.

Large Egyptian forces were massed on the Southern border. Rabbi Goren, who at the outset of the tense situation had been in Australia on a lecture tour of the Jewish community there, was called home. He immediately began to work to strengthen the morale of the soldiers on all fronts. He traveled to the Egyptian border, to be with the army on the Shabbat of *parshat Bamidbar.*

Two days later, on 26 *Iyar,* June 5, 1967, the Six Day War began. On the morning of the war's outbreak, Rabbi Goren wrote a special dispatch for the forces. He then took a small *sefer Torah* with him, and began to go to visit each and every battlefield unit. The soldiers at each of the stops greeted him warmly, kissed the Torah, and were fortified by his prayers and words of encouragement.

On the third day of the war, when on his way back to Jerusalem, his command car was hit by the Egyptians and set on fire. Rabbi Goren found cover in a field of wheat, which was also set on fire. The army rescued him. Rabbi Goren remained with the troops in the south for two days and then made his way north to Jerusalem. By this time, it was known that in the first hours of the war the Israeli Air Force had destroyed the Egyptian and Syrian air forces on the ground.

In Jerusalem, the Israeli forces under Major-General Uzi Narkiss had thwarted Jordanian efforts to take the city. Motta Gur's fifty-fifth brigade, which had initially been intended for the Egyptian front but was not needed, was called back to Jerusalem. Its task was to break through the area in the northern part of the city at Sheikh Jarrah, the Police School, and Ammunition Hill. These operations involved some of the most costly and difficult fighting of the war. The Jordanian forces were well entrenched and fought fiercely.

Rabbi Goren rushed back to Jerusalem. He stopped at the home of his father-in-law, the *nazir,* in order to borrow a *shofar* to replace his own that had been burned when his command car was hit in Gaza. Then he went to the Rockefeller Museum in East Jerusalem and the just-established command post of Mordechai Gur. There Rabbi Goren urged Mordechai Gur to keep his old promise of liberating the holy places and begin moving the troops toward the Old City. But Gur firmly resisted all persuasion, and would not go forward without a direct command from the General Staff.

According to the Israeli Army Encyclopedia (volume 16), the next morning Rabbi Goren was fearful that the historical opportunity to capture the Old City and establish Jewish control there for the first time in 2,000 years would be missed. He telephoned Dr. Yaakov Herzog, the director-general of the prime minister's office, and urged him to convince Prime Minister Eshkol, before the Cabinet meeting about to be convened that morning, to give the order to take the city. Herzog said he would do this.

On the following morning, the 28th of *Iyar*, June 7, 1967, the order to take the city was given. Rabbi Goren, who had barely slept for three days and three nights, was with the troops that moved toward the Lions Gate (St. Stephens Gate). He began the race from the Rockefeller Museum. The orders were to remain close to the walls because of the enemy fire. He had with him the *sefer Torah* that he took with him everywhere. This was a *sefer Torah* that had been dedicated in the name of Baruch Asher Shapira who had been killed in the War of Independence. Rabbi Goren ran with *shofar* and *sefer Torah* in hand in the direction of the Lions Gate in the Old City. When criticized after the war for unnecessarily endangering himself, Rabbi Goren told reporter Haggai Huberman that he ran in the middle of the road with the *sefer Torah* and *shofar* and knew he would not be hit. He said that his past experience, when he had prayed out on the ramparts of the Suez Canal in face of Egyptian fire, had proven this to him. Rabbi Goren said that in this fantastic race to the Lions Gate he felt as if he was flying to heaven. He believed the demonstration of fearlessness would be of inspiration to the soldiers.

At the Lion's Gate, Rabbi Goren began to blow the *shofar* and to pray out loud as the halacha requires in a time of war. After a long run, he came to the Temple Mount, where he began to pray Psalm 24, "The earth is the Lord's and the fullness thereof." And then he blew the *shofar* – *Tekia! Terua! Shevarim! Tekia!* – and read the manifest he had prepared that morning declaring that all the holy places are now open to people of all faiths. A short time earlier, at 10 a.m., Colonel Gur, the commander of the operation, had reached the Temple Mount and from there spoke the words that stirred Israel and the Jewish people throughout the world: "The Temple Mount is in our hands."

After an hour on the Temple Mount, Rabbi Goren went down to the Western Wall, which had begun to fill up with Israeli paratroopers. As the hour was early, Rabbi Goren said *Tehillim*; at 12:20 he could begin to pray the afternoon *Mincha* prayer. At the repetition of the *Amida*, Rabbi Goren inserted the *Nachem* prayer, which is usually said only on *Tisha B'Av*. But he changed the *nusach*, and instead of saying "the mourning city," he said "the liberated city, joyful and exultant, whose children have returned to her." After this, he said *Hallel Gadol* and made the blessing with *Shem* and *Malkhut*. Hundreds of soldiers, religious and not, joined in the saying of the *Hallel*.

A most moving description of this same event at the Kotel is given in Uzi Narkiss's book, *The Liberation of Jerusalem*.

> We made our excited way through the streets to the Mugrabi Gate, along a dim alley, turned right down a flight of steps, impatiently faced another right turn – and there it was: The Wailing Wall. I quivered with memory. Tall and awesome and glorious, with the same ferns creeping between the great stones, some of them inscribed.
>
> Silently, I bowed my head. In the narrow space were paratroopers, begrimed, fatigued, overburdened with weapons. And they wept. They were not "wailing at the Western Wall," not lamenting in the fashion familiar during the Wall's millenia of being. These were tears of joy, of love, of passion, of an undreamed first reunion with their ancient monument to devotion and prayer. They clung to its stones, kissed them, these rough battle-weary paratroopers, their lips framing the *Shema*.

Six Day War Chief Army Chaplain Shlomo Goren surrounded by soldiers, blows *shofar* in front of just liberated Western Wall, Jersualem, June 7, 1967. GPO, photographer David Rubinger.

But more exalted, prouder than all of them, was Rabbi Goren. Wrapped in a *tallit* (prayer shawl), blowing the ram's horn, and roaring like a lion: 'Blessed be the Lord God, Comforter of Zion and Builder of Jerusalem. Amen.' Suddenly he saw me, embraced me, and planted a ringing kiss on my cheek, a signal to everyone to hug and kiss and join hands. The rabbi, like one who had waited all his life for this moment, intoned the *Kaddish*, the *Kel Maleh Rachamim* in memory of those who had fallen to liberate the Temple Mount and Jerusalem, the City of the Lord: 'May they find their peace in Heaven. And let us say Amen.'

The restrained weeping became full-throated sobs, an uncurbed emotional outburst. Sorrow, fervor, happiness, and pain combined to produce this mass of grieving and joyous men, their cheeks wet, their voices unsteady. Again the *shofar* was blown: *tekiya* (a short, but unbroken sound) followed by the *shevarim* (a short but tremolo sound). And Rabbi Goren heralded, "This year, at this hour, in Jerusalem!"

During this time, Rav Goren sent a special army vehicle to bring his father-in-law, the *nazir*, and Rabbi Zvi Yehuda HaKohen Kook. Nineteen years before, the Nazir had vowed not to leave his home except for the purpose of going to pray at the liberated Temple Mount and Western Wall. Now he could at least leave his home.

The Jewish people had, in Defense Minister Moshe Dayan's words – which were to become a central article of the national faith – "returned to their holy places, never to be parted from them again." For the first time in 2,000 years, the most holy site of the Jewish people was in Jewish hands. The city, which had been divided was reunited again.

What had begun with the threat of the destruction of the Jewish state ended with the realization of a dream the Jewish people had fervently maintained for 2,000 years.

Surrounded by IDF soldiers, Rabbi Goren blows *shofar* at the *Kotel*, Jerusalem, June 7, 1967. GPO.

Rabbi Goren with soldiers reclaiming Holy Places in Jerusalem, June 7, 1967. From *Tzahal beCheilo, Army and Security Encyclopedia, Revivim* 16 (Maariv Ed).

Rabbi Shlomo Goren had long prepared for, and prayed for this moment. He understood its significance not simply as a moment in a nation's history, but as part of a worldwide process of redemption. For him, this great moment was a moment of deepest religious fulfillment.

Yet Rabbi Goren's prayers and actions, even at these moments of great exaltation, were not unmixed with pain and grief. Even on the day of greatest triumph, Rabbi Goren was weighed down with the pain of those who had lost loved ones.

When he returned home, exhausted, for the first time after the battle for Jerusalem, the first thing he did was find the addresses and phone numbers of, and set out to begin his visits of consolation to, the families of the fallen.

The nation and the people had been delivered, but 679 Israeli soldiers were killed in the war's battles and over 2,500 injured.

Chapter 17

TAKING RACHEL'S TOMB AND THE CAVE OF THE PATRIARCHS

The war did not end for Rabbi Goren with the taking of Jerusalem. There were other holy places, including the Tomb of Rachel outside Bethlehem, and the Machpelah Cave, the Cave of the Patriarchs, in Hebron. Rabbi Goren was also to play key roles in the liberation of these two holy sites.

After the survey and meeting with Colonel Gur on the Temple Mount, Rabbi Goren left the Old City area. He set out in the direction of Bethlehem and Hebron only to find traffic stopped near the Talpiyot area, as there were suspected minefields ahead. He also encountered there a large force of soldiers, and was told it would be a great deal of time before the road opened. So he returned to headquarters. After a few hours, he returned to Talpiyot. The road was now open, but clogged with vehicles.

Characteristically eager, and wishing to arrive at the holy sites first, Rabbi Goren had his driver turn on the siren, and they began going around the vehicles. At around 11:30 p.m. Rabbi Goren arrived at the Tomb of Rachel at the outskirts of Bethlehem. Rabbi Goren, Rabbi Menachem HaCohen, and the driver, Aryeh Shalom, were the first to enter the tomb. They did so only after breaking down one large door, and having the key to the internal door thrown to them by the Arab custodian. After praying, Rabbi Goren cried out the Biblical verse, "Our mother Rachel, Your children have returned to their borders."

From there, Rabbi Goren continued to Gush Etzion. He met there with the commander of the forces of the Jerusalem Brigade, and told him that he wished to speak to the soldiers before they made their scheduled move at 3:30 a.m. toward Hebron. The commander agreed to let Rabbi Goren address the soldiers. Rabbi Goren was placed up on a tank, and said, "I want to tell you what you are about to liberate today, and the kind of enemy you are going against. You are about to liberate the city that is second in its degree of holiness, the city of the Fathers, the city of the kingdom of David. And you are going to do battle against the worst murderers in this land, those who in cold blood killed 162 soldiers after those soldiers had raised a white flag and surrendered. You should know this. In the name of the Lord, go forth and triumph." (This is a translation of the text given in the Israeli Army Encylopedia from which this account is largely drawn.) Rabbi Goren then said the prayer before going out to battle with the soldiers.

He then set out in the direction of Hebron. He ordered his driver to travel at great speed, and to go around any traffic in front of them. So they passed the bulk of the brigade's force. They went around the tanks, and then around the jeeps of the Sayeret. Menachem HaCohen cautioned at this point, that they were out alone ahead of everyone else, but this did not deter Rabbi Goren. He suspected that others had gotten to Hebron first.

At 6 a.m., they arrived in Hebron. The citizens of the city were all closed in their houses, in great fear of retaliation. There were white flags everywhere. Rabbi Goren had a few shots fired in the air in order to announce to the city that the Israeli forces had arrived. A youngster raced toward the jeep. Rabbi Goren had him direct them toward the Cave of the Patriarchs.

The doors were locked, and only after the arrival of heavy army equipment were the gates opened. After entering, Rabbi Goren and his people prayed *Shacharit*. Rabbi Goren then blew the *shofar*. Rabbi Goren found two Arabs, one with a whole string of keys. Rabbi Goren appointed him to be a guard over the site, and ordered that no one should be allowed to enter the cave without the accompaniment of officers.

After this, two Arabs arrived and said that the mayor of the city wished to surrender. Rabbi Goren said an act of surrender is not done at a holy place, and said he and his men would go to the city hall for the surrender ceremony. The soldiers wanted to put the flag up on the city hall, but Rabbi Goren said the Cave of the Patriarchs is more important, and had it put up there.

Rabbi Goren then went to the city hall, where the Israeli commander of the operation, Zvika Opher, received the surrender from Mayor Jaabri in unconditional terms, as Rabbi Goren had insisted upon.

IDF Chief Rabbi Shlomo Goren at burial of remains of the last defenders of Massada, June 2, 1969. In photo (front row, left to right) Yigael Yadin, Menachem Begin, Zerach Warhaftig. GPO, photographer Moshe Milner.

On the steps of Hebron City Hall after official surrender had taken place, June 1967. Standing next to Rabbi Goren (right to left) Sheikh Jabri, Menachem HaCohen, Zvika Ofer. From *Tzahal beCheilo, Army and Security Encyclopedia, Revivim* 16 (Maariv Ed).

Chapter 18

FORBIDDING JEWISH PRAYER ON THE TEMPLE MOUNT

Rabbi Goren, in one long remarkable day, had been present and led the prayers at the holiest sites as they were returned to the Jewish people. In the weeks and months ahead, he would be responsible for administering these sites. This involved considerable cleaning and repair work, especially in the Tomb of Rachel, which had been cluttered with debris and neglected. Defense Minister Moshe Dayan ordered the main esplanade before the Western Wall be cleared and set up for religious services. In the weeks and months after the war, hundreds of thousands of Jews would stream to the reunited city of Jerusalem and to the holy sites elsewhere.

At the same time as this work of reconstruction was being done, a great controversy developed regarding the situation on the Temple Mount. This was in part due to the differing perceptions of Rabbi Goren and Defense Minister Dayan.

For Rabbi Goren, the Western Wall, at which Jews had prayed at for only 300 years, was an extremely important, but nonetheless, secondary, sight. The heart of Jewish longing for 2,000 years was not the Western Wall, but the *Beit HaMikdash* on *Har HaBayit*, the Temple on the Temple Mount. This is the place to which Jews all over the world directed their prayers, the very heart and center of Jewish reality. If Israel is the center of the Jewish people, and Jerusalem is the center of Israel, then the Temple Mount is the center of Jerusalem.

For Rabbi Goren, the victory of the Six Day War was not simply a historical event, but an event of religious significance in the deepest way, a turning point in the whole process of redemption. For Moshe Dayan, however great the historical meaning of the victory was, it was not primarily a religious event.

For Moshe Dayan, the center of Jewish longing was the Western Wall. The mosques, which had been on the Mount for 1,400 years, were the reality. To try to alter this in any way would, he thought, bring Israel into permanent conflict with the Islamic world, and would convert a largely national conflict into a religious one. Moshe Dayan's aim was to leave effective control of the mosques and the Temple Mount to the Muslims, avoiding any additional confrontation. It was also to create the goodwill for the "peace" he hoped might now come when the Arabs recognized that they could not defeat Israel on the battlefield. Moshe Dayan's considerations were aimed at bringing positive practical benefits to Israel historically and politically. Thus, his decision was to leave the Temple Mount – what for the Muslims was the Haraam-el-Sharif and the El-Aksa mosques – to the Muslims, and take for the Jews only the area below, the Kotel.

Rabbi Goren's position was that the Jews could not abandon their holiest place, and that a site of Jewish worship should be established on the Temple Mount. In August of 1967, he invited surveyors from the Israeli Engineering Corps to make a complete mapping of the Mount. This was done to help ensure that the areas on which Jews were forbidden to walk would be clearly delineated and so that an area could be designated where Jewish worship would be possible on the Mount without violation of any religious prohibition. From their measurements, it was clear that from the Mugrabi Gate south in the direction of El-Aksa mosque, the prohibition is less severe than from the Mugrabi gate north.

After the conquest of the Temple Mount, Rabbi Goren ordered the opening of a *beit midrash* in a building near the Mugrabi Gate, where half of it was on the Mount, and half off. In this building, Rabbi Goren organized religious conferences, *shiurim,* and lessons on *Har HaBayit.* In

August, Rabbi Goren heard rumors that Dayan intended to hand authority over the Temple Mount to the Wakf. He rapidly organized a conference of sympathetic supporters to resist this.

Rabbi Goren then made a plan to organize a prayer service of 50,000 people, which would take place on *Shabbat Nachamu*. In a prior, much smaller, service, fifty people had participated in a prayer service on *Tisha B'Av*. In this service, an ark was taken out, and placed in the middle open area before the steps leading to the Mosque of Omar. News of this had appeared in the newspapers and created a public storm.

On August 16, 1967, Chief of Staff Yitzhak Rabin sent a letter of reprimand to Rabbi Goren in which he instructed him that as a person in uniform he was obliged to follow orders, and could not, on his own initiative, take actions that would have political significance. The chief of staff ordered the cancellation of any intended prayer service. He forbade Rabbi Goren from holding any service in the area on Shabbat, except for one which would be held at the Kotel. He ordered that in the future any Jewish prayer services would be conducted in the area of the Western Wall, and not on the Temple Mount.

Rabbi Goren replied to these prohibitions with a letter of his own to the Ministerial Committee for the Safeguarding of Holy Places, in which he expressed his shock at being forbidden to conduct services on the Temple Mount. He was dismayed at the thought that the single place in the world where Jews would be forbidden to pray is the one most holy to them. Rabbi Goren was outraged at the thought that the security forces of Israel would turn away Jews from praying at their most sacred site. And with his characteristic scholarly rigor, he detailed instances in the past where Jews had prayed on the Mount. Rabbi Goren warned in his letter that Jewish history would not forgive this generation for such an action. He stated that there was no intention to do any harm to the Muslim places of worship. He reiterated that there was no halachic justification at this point, and no means for building a Third Temple on the site. He stated that this building could not be done until a prophetic presence appeared in the world. He pointed out that the government's action was a violation of its own law, which called for freedom of worship for all faiths.

The position of Moshe Dayan carried the day in the government. Jews, after their greatest historical victory on the battlefield, denied themselves their most sacred place of worship. In the years after, the Temple Mount became a place of Israeli military presence, but of ongoing humiliation of Judaism.

Jews were to be arrested for opening a siddur or book of Pslams there. Muslims on the Mount held hate-filled, political-religious rallies, from time to time violently attacked the Jews at the Kotel below, and illegally destroyed Jewish archaeological sites.

In subsequent decades, the vision of compromise promoted and instituted by Dayan, of Muslims up above, and Jews down below, did not bring peace. Instead the Muslims, who had been intimidated and shattered at the Jewish victory in 1967 became even more intolerant. Through the years they not only maintained their monopoly on prayer on the Temple Mount (a monopoly that was in direct contradiction to Israel's own mandate to permit freedom of worship in all holy places), but instituted actions aimed at erasing all signs of Jewish historical presence there. They built a vast new underground mosque.

Moreover, Israel's maintaining security on the Mount became an increasingly costly process as frequent Arab rioting led to world condemnation of Israeli measures of control. The worst incident occurred in the rioting of 1996, where Muslims up above stoned the Jews at the Kotel. In the subsequent violence, a number of Arab rioters were killed, and almost the whole world stood against Israel.

The Dayan plan led nowhere. It neither gave the Jews a rightful place of prayer on the Mount, nor created a more tolerant Muslim population. By giving in wholly to Muslim demands for exclusive control of religious worship on the Temple Mount, Dayan only encouraged the appetite to destroy every Jewish connection to the Mount, including traces of the past.

For his part, Rabbi Goren did not abandon the dream of Jewish prayer on the Mount. Each year, for as long as he was physically able, he would leave the Yom Kippur *davening* in Heichal Shlomo and walk to the special building, the Mahkameh, adjacent to the Temple Mount, where he would pray the concluding Yom Kippur service of *Ne'ilah*.

Chapter 19

JEWISH PRAYER AT THE CAVE OF THE PATRIARCHS: DAYAN VS. GOREN

Rabbi Goren did not succeed in convincing Defense Minister Dayan and the government of Israel of the rightness and necessity of Jewish prayer on the Temple Mount. He did, however, succeed in making certain that Jews would be able to pray in another holy site, the Cave of the Patriarchs in Hebron. Here too, Rabbi Goren's opponent was Moshe Dayan, whose very limited interest and knowledge of Jewish religious practice led him to think primarily in practical political terms.

Dayan would have had the Jews follow the discriminatory practice that had been invoked in the time that the British ruled, i.e., the Muslims would pray inside the tomb, and the Jews would have to pray at the steps outside. Under Muslim rule, the Jews had only been allowed to climb to the seventh step and look through a hole to the inside. They were not allowed to step in the building over the tomb itself.

In entering the tomb, Rabbi Goren had already violated Dayan's prohibition. Learning this, Dayan ordered Rabbi Goren, if he dared enter the tomb again, to take off his shoes as is the Muslim practice when entering a holy place. Rabbi Goren absolutely refused, insisting that in a Jewish holy place he, as a Jew, must follow the Jewish custom and habit. This time Dayan, perhaps understanding the historical injustice of barring Jews from their own holy place, conceded to Rabbi Goren's view.

Defense Minister Dayan had initially hoped that the Cave of the Patriarchs would become a place of pilgrimage for Jews. He had not wanted to complicate matters by having the tomb turned into a place of prayer. Nonetheless, upon seeing that Jews were coming to pray, he acceded to Rabbi Goren on this matter. After hundreds of years of exclusion, Jews were given access to the Cave of the Patriarchs.

Both Defense Minister Dayan and Rabbi Goren agreed on the question of allowing Muslims to continue to pray at the site. This was in accordance with the fundamental principle of both government and army policy that the holy sites should be accessible to those of all faiths.

Chapter 20

FROM THE ARMY TO TEL AVIV

In 1967 Rabbi Goren reached the climax of his career in terms of his prestige and popularity, and it could only be expected that a certain decline would follow. In a sense, this decline in the public's eyes came with the very disputes Rabbi Goren had with Moshe Dayan over the holy places. For many who saw Israel's path to peace and integration into the Middle East as coming through sacrifice of territories won in the Six Day War, Rabbi Goren represented a dangerous atavistic tendency, a possible spoiler of the whole process. He was often portrayed in the press as a kind of cranky, religious fanatic, arrogant and opinionated and rude. His positions were regarded by the political Left as backward and reactionary.

Rabbi Goren himself contributed to this decline in his prestige through a number of not particularly happy incidents. In one incident, around the Shavuot holiday immediately after the Six Day War, he tried to stage a kind of spectacle in the desert, an imitation of Moses receiving the Torah at Sinai. The Israeli public saw this act as an ego trip and waste of public funds.

In 1969, Rabbi Goren was chosen to be Chief Rabbi of Tel Aviv. He did not, however, enter the position until two years later. Everyone understood this to be a stepping stone, as it in fact proved to be one year later when Rabbi Goren was chosen to be chief Ashkenazi rabbi of Israel. Rabbi Goren, however, did not add to his stature by his seeming resentment towards his successor in the army rabbinate, and by criticizing him strongly during the Yom Kippur War. At one point he did this by calling in to a radio talk show, which did not particularly endear him in the eyes of the public. For many, a public official is supposed to have a special kind of standing and dignity.

In these incidents, the great Rabbi Goren, who would make any personal sacrifice for the good of the people of Israel, seemed to be replaced by an egocentric *ilui*, who put his own interests and standing before anything else.

Chapter 21

CHIEF RABBINATE

There was a great hope that upon Rabbi Goren's, and with him Rabbi Ovadia Yosef's, accession to the Chief Rabbinate in 1972, that there would be a restoration of prestige to the institution, which the great Rabbi Avraham Yitzhak HaKohen Kook had given it. These were, after all, two of the great *talmidei chachamim* of their generation, and also two of the great *poskim*, rabbis who make decisions based on Jewish law. Rabbi Goren was a great pioneer in all areas connected with halachic ruling in the army, and also in new areas of medical technology. Rabbi Ovadia had a unique status as the supreme Sephardi *posek* in every area of life.

Unfortunately, and the reasons for this are still subject to debate, the period of ten years in which they shared the Chief Rabbinate was marred by personal dispute between them. Many claim the real dispute was between their followers, especially from the inner circle who intrigued and maneuvered against each other. Whatever the reason, the public soon had the perception that each of the rabbis was more concerned about their own personal prestige than they were with the general well-being of the people of Israel.

The very fact of the controversy undermined one of Rabbi Goren's central aims. In all his work in the army rabbinate, and as a central tenet of his teaching, he had stressed the importance of the unity of the people of Israel. On assuming the office of Chief Rabbi, there was a public hope that Israel would enter a new period of spiritual unity and development.

Controversy and difficulty also entered from another quarter. Perhaps the most controversial case Rabbi Goren ever dealt with was one that had to do with the question of the religious status and Jewish legitimacy of a brother and sister, the Langers. Their legitimacy became a matter for the rabbinic courts when each of them applied to be married. The issue itself received tremendous publicity in Israel and seemed to be one that would put an inseparable barrier between the religious and secular publics.

This case was at the center of public attention in its time in Israel. It made many enemies for Rabbi Goren, especially in the hareidi community.

Rabbi Goren ruled that the children were legitimate, and the same day he published the ruling, he conducted the marriages of the brother and the sister to their respective spouses. He did not however publish the name of the other nine judges of the special rabbinic court he had convened to do this. This was because of the atmosphere of threat and intimidation that surrounded the case.

This case was one of many in which Rabbi Goren showed how faithfulness to halacha could lead to answering the needs of the community in the most humane way possible.

For the majority of the hareidi community, Rabbi Goren lost his standing with this case. True, it was another instance of his doing what he believed was right, putting his own name and reputation at risk. True, he made the humane decision. But the goal of being the Chief Rabbi of a unified Jewish people in Israel moved farther away with this case.

Controversy and division also played a central part in another area: the question of archaeological digs with regards to possible violation of the halacha and disturbance of the remains of Jews. Here, Rabbi Goren seemed to set himself in opposition to the world of academic research, the world of liberal progress. This was especially so when he identified as remains of Jews, certain bones in the Judean Desert, which many archaeologists argued were in no way connected to past Jewish communities.

Another area of controversy was the whole question of the settling and development of *Eretz Yisrael* beyond the Green Line, and the possible ceding of territory within Biblical Israel to the Arabs. Rabbi Goren was opposed by the great part of the academic and media establishment. His dedication to the whole of the Land of Israel made him, for many Israelis on the left of the political spectrum, a "wild irresponsible chauvinist."

So here, too, the goal of unifying and inspiring the people as a whole was elusive. And in the eyes of many, Rabbi Goren was not only *not* the source of unity, but was a particularly abrasive source of division and conflict within the society.

In his defense, though, he by no means created the conflicts his actions sometimes aggravated.

Nonetheless, instead of the Israeli people's admiration and love for him increasing during his tenure in the rabbinate, they became more alienated, including many who had admired him during his period as Chief Rabbi of the Israeli Army.

In this sense at least, it is difficult to see his tenure as Chief Rabbi as one of great success.

When he entered the office, his model and inspiration was his boyhood teacher and friend, the first Chief Rabbi of Israel, Rabbi Avraham Yitzhak HaKohen Kook.

Rav Kook also had a great deal of controversy and difficulty during his time in the Chief Rabbinate. He had suffered greatly from the abuse of many of the *old yishuv*, of the non-Zionist hareidim. But he was generally loved and admired. He was a symbol of the unity of Israel, who reached out to the primarily secular *yishuv*, and had many admirers from it. He was considered to be a figure of great love and humanity.

Despite Rabbi Goren's many good deeds and charity, his tremendous devotion to the well-being of each individual who he felt was in need, his deep love of *Am Yisrael*, and the considerable work he did while he was the Chief Rabbi, his public image suffered.

His great strength and conviction and his faith in his own rightness

Rabbi Goren blessing PM Menahem Begin while Rabbi Ovadia Yosef looks on.
GPO.

Chief Rabbis Shlomo Goren and Ovadia Yosef attending the 30th Zionist
Congress at Binyanei Hauma in Jerusalem, Dec. 6, 1982.
GPO, photographer Miki Shuvitz.

often came across as arrogance. The endless bickering with Rav Ovadia Yosef made them both seem petty in the eyes of many. He did not succeed in touching the broader Israeli public, inspiring them as he had succeeded in touching so many in the army through the years.

The controversy and difficulty of his tenure as Chief Rabbi of Israel continued throughout his term. True, the hostility between himself and Rav Ovadia diminished in their second term, especially when the question arose of whether their terms would be extended, and they would be permitted a third term. Their common struggle brought them together, but in the end their joint effort to have another term was rejected by the political establishment.

As the controversy over the additional term went on, again it seemed that Rabbi Goren was pursuing more of his own private interests than the public good. Also during this time, his meetings with many politicians, his whole relationship, especially with the leaders of the National Religious Party, was viewed closely in the newspapers in an unflattering way. Rabbi Goren felt that promises had been made to him that were broken. When at some point he contemplated forming a religious party of his own in place of the National Religious Party, this too was seen as an act of self-interest.

There were many other controversies, including those relating to the building of his yeshiva opposite the Kotel, and to the placing on its roof of a six-candled Agam sculpture memorializing those murdered in the Holocaust. Without going into the question of the relative rightness or wrongness of Rabbi Goren's actions, it is possible to say that the controversies themselves damaged his reputation. For it is one thing to be seen as a tough, feisty fighter for the nation and its well-being, and another to be perceived as a fighter only for one's own private position and projects.

Many of Rabbi Goren's friends will argue that his tenure in the Chief Rabbinate strengthened the institution, raised the level of the

Rabbi Goren in receiving line with Golda Meir, American ambassador Barber, Yigael Allon, Abba Eban, and Shlomo Hillel, waiting to receive President Shazar returning from Washington, Jan. 9, 1973.
GPO, photographer Fritz Cohen.

Rabbi Goren with Patriarch Justinian I of Bucharest at the office in Heichal Shlomo, Jerusalem, May 22, 1975. GPO, photographer Yaakov Sa'ar.

religious courts, and halachic ruling in general. However, there is no doubt that the great promise of Rabbi Goren's candidacy, unifying the people of Israel, moving the public as a whole closer to the Torah, bringing about of a society more firm in its devotion to the Land of Israel, was not realized.

Rabbi Goren at work in his office at Heichal Shlomo, Jerusalem, June 22, 1988. Photographer: Joel Fishman.

Chapter 22

LAST YEARS

Rabbi Goren fought for a third term as Chief Rabbi. But political forces beyond his control dictated his defeat. He did not take this defeat easily. He had a strong sense that he was the right person for the position and that he had the halachic authority, the knowledge of the broader society, and the moral courage that no one else had. His loss embittered him, and he could not show special graciousness to his successor any more than he had been able to show real graciousness to his successor as chief army rabbi.

Again he contemplated forming a religious party of his own. But his wife and family were firmly against this. Also friends like Rabbi Alfassi advised against it. The truth was he did not have the same kind of mass following as did his Sephardi counterpart, Rav Ovadia Yosef. Moreover, many of his friends and family felt that as an outspoken lover of truth and a man who invariably said what he really believed, he was not made for the world of political intrigue and broken promises.

The loss of position created an entirely new situation for Rabbi Goren. For the first time in over thirty-five years he was without an official position. Even the small things bothered him. He was without a car, a driver, a personal secretary. He had to run and do errands by himself, and complained of having to go to the post office for himself. These complaints were made because the time was taken from Torah study.

Rabbi Goren had been in the center of public attention for many many years when he was forced to step down from the Chief Rabbinate.

While public interest in his thought, and most especially his halachic ruling on items on the public agenda, never disappeared, there was a decline in interest in him. He was still on the stage, but no longer on center stage.

This was difficult for him because, as his long-time assistant, Menachem HaCohen, said, he was a person who "loved the action" and wanted to be in the center of it. Ideally as a *talmid chacham*, Rabbi Goren might have been expected to forget the world of public life and its controversies and devote himself to his Torah projects. After all, his great dream of editing a new and completely annotated edition of the *Yerushalmi* had been delayed for many years. Indeed he did, during these years, work on his writings more than he had previously.

But at times he seemed to flounder, seemed to be searching for a role in the public mind. He did not, however, stray far from controversy. In the last months of his life, he made the ruling that, in one sense, seemed to violate much of what he had stood for throughout his life. He ruled that soldiers had a moral duty to disobey orders if ordered to evacuate Jewish settlements. Here he said he was doing nothing different from what he had always done: giving his first loyalty and priority to the teaching of the Torah. However, he was ordering a subversion of the authority of the Jewish state, something he had not ever done in such a blunt way before. It should be mentioned that on a matter so fundamental to his whole worldview as the right of Jews to pray on the Temple Mount, he had never called for active rebellion against the State.

In any case, the great disappointment of Oslo, his feeling that his friend, Yitzhak Rabin, betrayed the principles they had lived and fought for, and his sense that the great redemptive action of liberating the Land of Israel was being reversed, caused him tremendous anguish and pain. The country he loved and dedicated his life to was seemingly moving against the very principles on which it had been founded. Giving parts of the Holy Land to another people was in itself an abomination, but giving it, as he

Chief Rabbi Goren lighting the first light of Hannukah with son of Prisoner of Zion Lein Hanoch, Dec. 24, 1978. GPO, photographer Yaacov Sa'ar.

Rabbi Goren with Prime Minister Yitzhak Shamir at the dedication of his Ha'Idra Yeshiva in the Old City, Jerualem. Phographer: Joel Fishman.

saw it, to terrorist murderers was an act of breaking all the vessels. In this sense his extreme reaction to this was no surprise. For he felt that all he had lived and struggled for was being placed in great danger.

In these years out of power, Rabbi Goren made important trips to Poland and to the United States, and he served as ambassador-at-large for the Jewish people. He continued to work in many areas, especially in halachic responsa. He wrote a major work, *Har HaBayit*, on the Temple Mount. He continued to serve as rabbi in Kommemiyut Avraham, the congregation he had founded in Tel Aviv and named after his father. He saw his family grow and grandchildren born. He continued to be in contact with his many friends, and his irrepressible spirit brought life and interest wherever he went. His enormous intellectual energy remained with him and he kept himself abreast of all the latest technological developments, especially in the area of biotechnology, where he was frequently called upon to give responsa.

During these years, Rabbi Goren worshipped in the synagogue in North Tel Aviv. His successor there, Rabbi Yitzhak Alfassi, speaks of the great spirit and joy which Rabbi Goren brought to this congregation. Rabbi Goren was the kind of person who did everything with all his heart and soul and might, and was on all accounts a remarkable *ba'al tefillah*, not to speak of *maggid shiur*. His love of singing and dancing gave a special uplift to the celebrations and *smachot* of the congregation, and his tremendous energy and spirit in learning made the Torah taught and learned in this congregation of special value.

This congregation, which was in walking distance of the Goren home, was only one of the centers of Rabbi Goren's spiritual activity, but it was one he took a special delight in when he could be there.

The heart attacks he suffered tested his great determination and strength. However strong his will and fighting spirit, the limitations imposed by physical weakness took their toll on his total work output. He never did get to work on the *Yerushalmi* as extensively as he had hoped. So too, the plans he had for many books were left interrupted, though he did

Chief Rabbi Shlomo Goren in a thoughtful mood, Oct. 15, 1972.
GPO, photographer Fritz Cohen.

leave enough material for a whole set of books that were brought out in his name posthumously.

After a third heart attack in late 1994, he was hospitalized once again. On *erev Shabbat*, the family gathered in the hospital. They davened *Ma'ariv* using the traditional tunes that he loved.

Rabbi Goren made *Kiddush* for them.

It was to be his last act of blessing in a life of devotion and love to his family and to *Am Yisrael*.

At two o'clock that night he left this world. His death came sixty years to the day of the publication of his first work on Maimonides, on October 29, 1994 (24 *MarCheshvan* 5754).

In those sixty years he had done more than anyone could possibly have dreamed to help establish the existence and forge the identity and institutions of the new Jewish state.

THOUGHT AND CHARACTER

POLITICAL AND RELIGIOUS

Chapter 23

Rabbi Goren's Worldview

In one central sense it is somewhat misleading to speak of the worldview of Rabbi Goren as if this were his own individual creation. Rabbi Goren's view on the most fundamental issues of life and belief were Torah views. They were grounded deeply in his learning and in his dedication to a halachic way of life. Whenever he presented his view of a subject – whether in the form of an essay or halachic ruling, he always based his views on passages of Torah. In other words, Rabbi Goren's views were not mere inventions of his own mind or intellectual position. What he did when he was thinking and writing and presenting his views was to aim to present what he believed to be the truth of the matter. In his mind, this truth was not just *his* truth, but a universal truth.

In this sense, Rabbi Goren lived in an intellectual universe, and through a way of seeing things that was deeply opposed to the secular-modern, and most especially post-modern way of seeing things. He felt that his worldview was not one of many or a view relatively right for him; it was a worldview that presented the one Truth there is. It was, first and above all, a God-given truth, a truth of revelation and not one of pure reason alone. It was the historical, religious truth given to the people of Israel.

The strength and definiteness of Rabbi Goren's presentation of his views was very much connected with this force of inner conviction that he was affirming the Divine truth through his scholarship. No doubt, this in part explains his great difficulty with incorporating or understanding opposing non-Torah ways of addressing life's fundamental issues. The force of Rabbi Goren's conviction is also related to his having a clear idea of the role of the halachic teacher, the rabbi, the Jewish spiritual leader. The views he expounded were not expounded as part of a theoretical intellectual enterprise, a pure work of abstraction. Rather they are presented as part of his own effort and struggle to serve God and Israel. Rabbi Goren expounded his view on any question or subject in order to move the implicit program of action inherent in the understanding of the subject. If he was writing to convince his readers about the sanctity of the Land of Israel, he was doing it also so that they would help participate in sanctifying and redeeming the Land. His views, in other words, were geared to inspiring action.

Rabbi Goren believed that the Jew, most especially, was placed on this earth not for himself alone, but rather to serve God. Rabbi Goren's searching for, finding, and presenting the truth on any subject was part of his own effort to help bring about the Redemption. In this sense, as a thinker, he lived in a world in which thought and action did not exist in separate realms, but rather were related all the time. The passion of his thought and way of seeing things is also the passion of his action in living in accordance with his halachic picture of the world.

Chapter 24

A Redemptive Vision of Modern Jewish History

The view of the world held by Rabbi Goren is the view of a considerable minority of the Jewish people today. Perhaps the most outstanding figure in the modern exposition of this way of seeing the world is Rabbi Goren's mentor and friend Rabbi Avraham Yitzhak HaKohen Kook. Like Rav Kook, Rabbi Goren believed that a central redemptive action of human history is the return of the Jewish people to the Land of Israel. For both Rabbis Kook and Goren this is not a local or a Jewish event only, but an event of cosmic significance.

Modern secular Zionists championed return to the Land of Israel while abandoning traditional Jewish religious life. Anti-Zionist hareidim argue that such return is a provocative religious violation. Religious Zionists believe that returning to and building the Land is a Divine historical imperative. The Religious Zionist view is a synthesis that has Torah at its basis, and that urges redemption of the people of Israel through their return to the Land of Israel where they will live and fulfill the Torah of Israel.

It is impossible to understand Rabbi Goren's thought without understanding that with every fiber of his being he was inspired by this aspiration to human and Divine redemption. For him the State of Israel was not merely a place of refuge, or a new historical beginning away from persecution – the State of Israel in itself is a source of sanctity. The building of the state was not a simple practical act, but rather the realization of a religious vision. For Rabbi Goren, settling in, living in, and

95

building the Land of Israel are central to the living of a Torah way of life. For Rabbi Goren, as for the Ramban long before him, the Jew can only live a fully holy life while serving God in the Land of Israel.

In this sense, Rabbi Goren's pioneering, prolonged, and painstaking work in establishing the halachic basis for life in the Jewish army were acts of helping bring this redemptive vision of reality into being.

Chapter 25

The Land of Israel According to Halacha

For Rabbi Goren, Jewish sovereignty in the Land of Israel and the Jewish connection with *Eretz Yisrael* cannot be subsumed to the kind of European nation-state nationalism so prevalent in the nineteenth and twentieth centuries. For Rabbi Goren, the Jewish connection with Israel is not only a religious value, it is a basis of the Torah itself. In his work on *parshat hashavu'a*, Rabbi Goren taught that the first meeting of God with Abraham in the Torah already revealed this. For Rav Goren the first *mitzva* given to Abraham in Haran is *yishuv Eretz Yisrael*, the settling of *Eretz Yisrael* – and upon this all, everything else is based. The first promise is "to your seed will be given this Land." Later on, Rabbi Goren taught that in the meeting with Lot, Abraham is told to look in all directions and see the land that will be given to him and his descendants forever.

Thus, as Rabbi Goren believed, in Abraham's first meetings with God there are given not only the promise to the land and the extent of its borders, but the first and most basic *mitzva,* that of settling the Land of Israel.

Chapter 26

SETTLING *ERETZ YISRAEL*

Rabbi Goren cites the Rambam who teaches that the *mitzva* of settling *Eretz Yisrael* may be placed over and against all the other *mitzvot* combined. And in one sense his whole life can be seen as working to help realize this *mitzva*. This started with his family as a child in Kfar Hasidim, and continued all through his life, including his last years when he was such a strong defender of the settlements in Judea, Samaria, and Gaza.

Chapter 27

The Jewish State: Between Exile and the Messianic Age

Rabbi Goren divided Jewish history after the people of Israel's post-Sinai entrance into the Land of Israel into three periods. The first period in which he includes the time of both the First and the Second Temples (with a brief interruption of seventy years of exile) is the period within the Land. For one part of this period – the First Temple era – it is likely that a majority of the Jewish people were in the Land of Israel, while it is known that during the longer Second Temple period, the majority of Jews were outside the Land. Rabbi Goren indicates that they were nonetheless still considered part of the community of Israel, of the Jewish nation. In his view, there can be no Jewish national entity outside of the Land of Israel.

The second period of Jewish history is that which comes with the fall of the Second Temple. This is the period of exile in which Jews are driven from the Land of Israel, in which the great majority live outside the Land, and there is no Jewish power or rule within the Land.

For Rabbi Goren, this period of exile ended in 1948 with the creation of the modern state of Israel. However the exact definition and meaning of this transition is a subject of controversy. Rabbi Goren did not adopt the view of many Religious Zionists and speak of this period as the beginning of the Redemption. He does not claim it to be the clear and definite beginning of the Messianic era.

His understanding of the period, an understanding largely taken from his reading of the *Talmud Yerushalmi*, is that the period is an intermediate one between the Exile and the Messianic era. As Rabbi Goren understands it, the *Talmud Yerushalmi* indicates that an independent Jewish political entity and the building of the Temple will take place before the actual advent of the Messianic era. The actual reestablishment of the House of David and the true beginning of the Messianic era, which are the true beginning of the third phase of Jewish history, will come after the Temple and the state are in place.

This means that for Rabbi Goren it is not correct to consider the creation of the State of Israel as the sign that the Messianic era is already here. It is rather the indication that should certain conditions be met – the achievement of true Jewish sovereignty in the Land, the majority of Jewish people dwelling within Israel, the building of the Temple – that the Messianic era will come soon thereafter.

Chapter 28

RELIGIOUS SIGNIFICANCE OF THE STATE OF ISRAEL

Rabbi Goren often pointed out that his opponents from the secular Left and from the religious far Right were united in one thing: the denial of all religious significance and meaning to the State of Israel. For Rabbi Goren, this position was a denial of a fundamental truth of history and reality. As someone who fought to bring the Jewish state into being, it had meaning beyond the political. Israel, as he saw it, came into being not primarily as the result of a secular national people's liberation movement, but as a result of a Divine process. For Rabbi Goren, the coming into being of Israel was the realization of a part of the Divine plan.

For Rabbi Goren, the concept of "nation" has meaning for the Jews only within the Land of Israel. No matter how many millions of Jews live outside Israel in a particular community, such a community has, for him, no real national status.

In affirming the special religious status of the nation that came into being in 1948, Rabbi Goren found himself with many opponents within the hareidi world. The Rebbe of Lubavitch claimed that redemptive work should be done by the *Mashiach*, like building the Temple and fighting for the Land, so that in a sense the fight that the Jews made to establish the Land has no real halachic status. On the other hand, Rabbi Goren, relying on the *Talmud Yerushalmi*, saw the coming into being of an Israelite kingdom, or an independent state, as a sign that we have left the Age of Exile. This does not mean that Rabbi Goren felt that we have truly entered the Age of Redemption. But it does mean that there is great religious significance to the coming into being of the State.

The coming into being of the State of Israel marks a critical stage in the revival of the Jewish people according to Rabbi Goren, as it enables the promised return of the great majority of Jews to the Land. The fact of Jewish sovereignty, as he understood it, is a vital preliminary to the coming into being of the Messianic age

The State does not signal, according to Rabbi Goren, that the Messianic age has arrived, but it does signal that we have left the Age of Exile and are closer to the true Redemption than we have been in the past 2,000 years.

Chapter 29

Jewish Right to Sovereignty in all of *Eretz Yisrael*

For Rabbi Goren, Jewish sovereignty in the Land of Israel is a central part in the plan of divine history. Jewish sovereignty is not a contingent, practical matter – one that is open to ordinary political argument and discussion – but one that is inherent in the very structure of God's world. The Land of Israel is the land that has been promised to the Biblical forefathers. Only in the Land of Israel can the Jews live out their central historical mission as chosen people creating a Torah way of life and Torah society. For Rabbi Goren, there can really be no Jewish community outside Israel. The fulfillment of key *mitzvot* is impossible outside the Land of Israel.

In his polemic newspaper work, Rabbi Goren frequently cited the *mitzva* that prohibits transmitting sovereignty over the Land of Israel to a foreign power. He often invoked the view of the *Talmud Yerushalmi*, which says that *Eretz Yisrael* is the foundation of the Jewish faith, and that therefore, the sanctity of mankind is connected with the holiness of the Land.

Chapter 30

HALACHIC STATUS OF JUDEA AND SAMARIA

For Rabbi Goren, the conquest in 1967 of Judea and Samaria should have been followed ideally by their annexation to the State of Israel. As he understood it, the failure to make Judea and Samaria legally part of the State of Israel was more than simply a historical mistake, it was a violation of the Torah. Here Rabbi Goren based himself on the Ramban. According to Rabbi Goren, each day that we did not annex these areas to Israel we committed a violation of a positive *mitzva*. Rabbi Goren cites Ramban's injunction against leaving the land barren, or transmitting it to a foreign rule. Ramban insists that it is a positive *mitzva* for each and every generation to possess the land.

Morever, Rabbi Goren argues that while the Rambam does not share the Ramban's view on the settling of the land as a *mitzvah*, he does maintain that once we have conquered the Land in an act of self-defense – in a *milchemat mitzva* – we are then forbidden to abandon the Land.

Chapter 31

RABBI GOREN'S OPPOSITION TO A PALESTINIAN-ARAB STATE

Rabbi Goren had theological, historical, and practical existential reasons for his absolute opposition to ceding land in order to make a non-Jewish, Palestinian-Arab state in the Land of Israel. Above all, was the fidelity to the Covenant in which God promised the Land of Israel to the people of Israel.

But Rabbi Goren also based his opposition on historical argument. He frequently pointed out that in all the time the Jews had not had sovereignty on the Land, no other inhabitant nation had succeeded in creating a true independent nation here. Rabbi Goren also believed that the creation of another state in Judea and Samaria, which is the heartland of Biblical Israel, would constitute a constant threat and danger to the very existence of Israel. He often asserted that such a state would be a center of hatred and terror against Israel.

Unfortunately his sense of what would happen if the Jews ceded their historical homeland has been borne out in the years since the 1993 Oslo agreement. The Palestinian Authority, which for the international community is the governing body for a Palestinian-Arab state, has embodied the kind of enemy Rabbi Goren wanted to prevent.

His great despair at the Oslo agreement, which he saw as the betrayal of fundamental Jewish religious principles, most probably contributed to the illness that was to take his life.

Chapter 32

OSLO BETRAYAL

In the weekly newspaper opinion pieces that appeared in the *Jerusalem Post*, Rabbi Goren wrote of what he believed were elements of betrayal in the Oslo agreement of September 1993. The most apparent was the Jewish ceding of their right to the Promised Land and the recognition of another people's right to part of the land. This was, in Rabbi Goren's eyes, a betrayal of the Torah, a betrayal of God's promise to the Jewish people, and a betrayal of the Jewish people and the Land of Israel.

Another significant element of the betrayal was the transferring of weapons to those who had only moments before been enemies, and who had committed horrible acts of terror against the Jewish people. This miscarriage of justice had behind it a conception that proved to be not simply absurd, but extremely costly. It was that these terrorists would then become the defenders of the Jewish people and would fight to prevent any acts of Arab violence against the Jewish people.

Rabbi Goren's disappointment was made even more painful by the realization that Yitzhak Rabin, who embodied the idea of Jewish defense, had signed this agreement. A long-time Goren friend and companion through many campaigns, including that of the Six Day War, Rabin seemingly sacrificed the principle upon which he had lived his life: that Jews would rely only upon themselves for their defense. This was, for Rabbi Goren, a painful betrayal, which pushed him closer to the sense that secular Zionism had become bankrupt – and it thus pushed him, perhaps for the first time, toward making a halachic ruling that could contradict and supersede the authority of the State of Israel. When asked about whether soldiers should violate orders and refuse to evacuate settlements, he answered in a way that many interpreted to be defiant of the State's authority. He said that the settlement of the Land of Israel is a sacred principle, a commandment no one has the right to violate. Later he went even further than this, and when the second Oslo withdrawal was approved only with the aid of Arab members of Knesset, he ruled that valid decisions on vital matters of the Jewish state required a Jewish majority. For this, he was branded a racist and vilified in the media.

When asked about making peace with arch-terrorist Arafat, Rabbi Goren said in 1993 that every adult Jew had the moral duty, if he had the opportunity, to kill Arafat. This, too, won him much condemnation.

Here one might be tempted to note that Rabbi Goren, no longer in a position of public authority and responsibility, was free to express a kind of extremism he had not expressed before. But such an explanation seems farfetched when one considers that Rabbi Goren told what he thought to be "hard and unpleasant truths" all his life.

The better explanation may be found in the fact that Goren, like many others, saw Israel, in signing the Oslo agreement, as being untrue to itself, violating its own reason for being. His reactions were his own way of trying to halt this process, and even reverse it. And he did talk much about the need for Israel to take back those places in Judea, Samaria, and Gaza that had been relinquished in the wake of the Oslo Accords.

Chapter 33

PEACE AS AN ULTIMATE JEWISH IDEAL

Opponents of Rabbi Goren who did not trouble to probe the depth of his thought, accused him of being a militant and a warmonger. In fact, the idea of peace was central to his thought. For him, peace was the ultimate Jewish ideal, which could come only at the end of a long process of striving. He often noted that most Jewish prayers, including the central one of the *Amida* (silent prayer), do not begin with, but end with a call for peace. For him the whole notion of Redemption and a Messianic age in history is bound up with a world that has come to true peace.

Rabbi Goren did not, however, believe that such a peace could be attained by compromising other ideals. He was especially troubled about the possible forfeiting of Jewish sovereignty over the whole of the Land of Israel. As he saw it, any partial solution or answer, any ceding of the Land of Israel to foreign sovereignty would create a situation of perpetual instability in which there could be no true peace. Peace as he understood it could come only when the people of Israel were realizing and fulfilling the Will of God and settling and building all the Land of Israel.

Chapter 34

Unfortunate Hour of his Leaving

In a sense, it is tragic that Rabbi Goren left this world at a time when so much that he had fought for, and dedicated his life to, seemed in danger. Instead of leaving the world at some great point of historical success for the Jewish people, he left it at the time when the Oslo agreement was going into effect. He left as parts of the Land of Israel that he helped redeem in 1967 were being transmitted to not only a foreign power, but to an enemy. This appeared in contradiction to the whole path of his life, where it seemed moments of great personal success and well-being had coincided with great redemptive actions for the people as a whole.

HAR HABAYIT: THE TEMPLE MOUNT

Chapter 35

BUILDING THE TEMPLE

After the Israeli Army captured the Temple Mount in June 1967, speculation began about rebuilding the Temple. While Rabbi Goren advocated Jewish prayer on the Temple Mount and conducted a service there in an area that he had marked as not prohibited to Jews for visiting, he did not advocate the actual rebuilding of the Temple, for he understood well enough the political dangers of any effort at removal of the mosques. Moreover, theologically he believed that we do not have the prophetic and halachic information that would enable us to construct the Temple. Thus, he believed that the construction of the Third Temple is incumbent upon the coming of a prophet who would teach the boundaries, the location of the Altar, the pedigree of priests who are to do the sacrificial service in the Temple, and the design of the building structure. Consequently, his position, which was often misinterpreted, was that it is not for us to take immediate action and begin once again the construction of the Temple. Rather, the Jewish people should assume a presence and establish a place of Jewish prayer on the Temple Mount, in a location permitted today for Jews to visit.

Chapter 36

Jewish Prayer on the Temple Mount

Rabbi Goren expected that one of the fruits of the victory of the 1967 war would be the restoration of Jewish prayer on the Temple Mount. Shortly after the victory, he did conduct a service on the Temple Mount. To his great shock and disappointment, the decision of Defense Minister Moshe Dayan – and later the decisions of the Israeli government's Ministerial Committee on the Holy Places, dated August 13, 1967 – to not permit such prayer, caused Rabbi Goren deep distress.

It meant that the government was not only casting away the fruit of its victory, but creating a situation that would be a source of sorrow for generations.

Rabbi Goren felt that the opening of the Temple Mount to Jewish prayer and to prayer for all people would not only put an end to the discrimination of exclusively Muslim prayers on the Mount, but would be a fulfillment of Biblical prophecy of Jewish return. He proposed that prayer could be done in open areas without in any way impinging upon the Muslims.

In the time since Defense Minister Dayan transmitted to the Wakf exclusive religious control on the holy mountain, the situation of discrimination has worsened. There has been a persistent effort on the part of the Muslims to not only deny Jewish access to the Temple Mount, but to destroy valuable archaeological materials that give proof of Jewish historical presence.

Rabbi Goren's instinctive understanding that the refusal to exercise Jewish rights would not lead to a status quo peace, but would instead further undermine the Jewish position, has proven prophetic.

Chapter 37

THE TEMPLE MOUNT ACCUSATION

Whenever there is a discussion about religious extremism in relation to the holy places in Jerusalem, and most especially in relation to the Temple Mount, there is one accusation repeatedly made against the Jewish people. The accusation is that at the taking of the Temple Mount in 1967, the then-Chief Rabbi of the army, Major-General Shlomo Goren suggested that the mosques on the Temple Mount be blown up. This accusation was first prominently published in a posthumously published interview with Major-General Uzi Narkiss (*Ha'aretz,* Dec. 31, 1997). It has become one of the most repeated sources for proving that there is a major Jewish extremist movement that intends to deprive the Muslim world of what for it is a central place of religious worship. The report claimed that Narkiss requested the interview be published posthumously.

There is, however, strong circumstantial evidence suggesting Rabbi Goren never made such a demand. First of all, there is a great deal that is problematic in the appearance of the original story. The first such problem is the alleged request that the story be published shortly after Narkiss died. The only other party involved in the story, Rabbi Goren, had died three years before in 1994. It seems very odd that Narkiss, who was a friend and admirer of Goren in 1967, would have made a charge against him that Goren would not have an opportunity to respond to. It would seem even more problematic that Narkiss wanted the story published only after he himself passed away.

There are other suspect elements about Narkiss's alleged accusation. Why did Narkiss wait for so many years to publish a story if he believed it so important? And why did he not include it in his two books, both of which touched upon the subject, *The Liberation of Jerusalem* and *Soldier of Jerusalem?* In those books, and most especially in the one which dealt at length with the liberation of the Western Wall and the Temple Mount, Narkiss not only did not show hostility toward Rabbi Goren, he instead wrote of him as one of the heroes of the story.

There is something suspect in the long delay, and the failure to give a longtime comrade a chance to respond. There is also something suspect in the reluctance to engage in any critical dialogue on the subject.

What is even more suspicious is the fact that Narkiss, in the original recounting of the events of 1967, told a completely different story and had a wholly positive relationship with Rabbi Goren. In *The Liberation of Jerusalem*, he wrote in an extremely adulatory way about Rabbi Goren. One of the six photos in the book is of Rabbi Goren and General Narkiss hugging each other in celebration of the great victory of the day.

The spirit of his relationship with Rabbi Goren can be indicated by Narkiss's description of his meeting with Goren as he was racing toward the Kotel and Temple Mount on the morning of June 7, 1967.

"We went back to the cars, abandoning the slow-moving half-tracks, and sped off in jeeps. Ahead, on the road from the valley to the Lion's Gate, was a column of paratroopers, led by General Rabbi Shlomo Goren, chief army chaplain, a *sefer Torah* under his arm, a *shofar* in his left hand, his beard bristling like the point of a spear, and his face bathed in perspiration. He was panting.

"Rabbi," I called out, "come aboard. We're going to the same place."

"No," he replied, "To the Temple Mount one goes on foot."

"Then we'll meet there." The jeep sprang forward.

The meeting on the Temple Mount, which took place shortly after, was described by Narkiss as follows:

"We ran towards Motta Gur, standing on the Mount where the flag of Israel flew. We were joined first by Moshe Stempel, Motta's deputy, and then by Rabbi Goren. We embraced and the rabbi prostrated himself and genuflected towards the Holy of Holies. In a resonant voice, he recited the ancient "Prayer to Battle":

> Hear O Israel, ye approach this day unto battle against your
>   enemies;
> let not your hearts faint, fear not, and do not tremble,
> neither be ye terrified because of them;
> for the Lord your God is He that goeth with you,
> to fight for you against your enemies to save you.
> (Deuteronomy 20: 3–4).

Hastily, I visited the mosque and was delighted to find no damage, except to a glass door, from the brief battle in the courtyard. As the cleaning up continued, I told Motta once again to make sure that no holy places or shrines were touched."

Narkiss's account is pervaded by a spirit of admiration for the special role Rabbi Goren played in the liberation of the city. It does not hint even in the slightest way that Rabbi Goren proposed doing damage to the mosques.

Now it might be suggested that the omission was deliberate because he did not think it was important at the time.

It might also be suggested that Rabbi Goren did say something like this, but that Narkiss, for patriotic reasons, understanding the great damage to Israel that would be done by the publication of the story, decided not to speak about it. But if that were the case, how do we explain his change of heart after so many years? Did Uzi Narkiss, who gave his life to the service of the people and State of Israel, suddenly overnight decide that he posthumously needed this accusation to be made public? And to do this when his long-time comrade and fellow-in-arms, Rabbi Goren, was no longer alive to respond to it?

Moreover, even if it were clearly and certainly established that Uzi Narkiss made this accusation against Rabbi Goren, the question would remain of why it was accepted as the truth by the world. Why was the world, or certain influential parts of it, interested in believing this accusation, when it was by no means proven? And why has it since become a "fact" that people "know" to be true and is accepted unchallenged everywhere?

The interview containing the allegation was published in *Ha'aretz* two weeks after Uzi Narkiss's death, and was translated and published in part on the very same day by the Associated Press. Since then, the accusation has had a considerable and nefarious history. The Left in Israel has used it as a weapon against the Right. It has been repeated countless times by columnists interested in proving a Jewish fanaticism equal to Arab fanaticism. It has been prominently featured in important intellectual journals, such as the *New York Review of Books*, the *New Republic*, and the *Jerusalem Report*. The accusation has been repeated many times as if it is a simple, well-established, and proven fact.

Anti-Semitic groups of the extreme right and left in Europe and the United States, including those who disseminate their hate on the Internet, have also made use of the story.

But the most damaging use of the accusation is by extremist Islamic groups, and particularly those within Israel itself. Extremists feed on the extremist statements of the other side. But the Islamic world is known especially for its capacity to hysterically distort any hint of threat from the other side. At the same time, there is an increasing sense that the Islamic world as a whole has difficulty with recognizing and giving respect to the religious rights of the other. Certainly the kinds of distortions of history like Arafat's famous denial that there ever was a Jewish Temple on the Mount, are quite commonplace, not only in everyday, but also scholarly, Muslim thought. In fact, in recent years there has developed a whole new movement of Islamic scholarship denying that the Temple ever existed. This is in contradiction to a long tradition of Islamic recognition of the fact of the Temple's existence.

Still, it is one thing to not recognize the other, and another to feel immediately and tremendously threatened by them. The story of Rabbi Goren's wishing to blow up the mosque has fueled the radical Islamic imagination.

The increasing Muslim fervor around the Temple Mount in recent years emphasizes the underlying assymetry on the whole question of the Temple Mount between the Islamic and the Jewish worlds. For what the Islamic world has always demanded is complete and exclusive control of the Temple Mount. There is a minority of religious Jews who have been debating among themselves whether it might be possible to build a small synagogue in which to worship in some corner of the Mount, far from where the Holy of Holies might have been. However, there is no real awareness on the part of the Islamic world of the actual, very limited demands most of the Jewish world has in regard to actual present-day worship on the Temple Mount. Similarly, the intellectual and political elite of the Islamic world have not related with seriousness to the Jewish origins of the holiness of the site.

All this may at first seem incidental to the alleged charge made against Rabbi Goren, but it connects to it when we consider what happened in the days following the taking of the Temple Mount in 1967. Once again, for Rabbi Goren, the most shocking and disappointing aspect of the 1967 War was the action taken by Moshe Dayan a few days after the war had ended. Dayan, who had initially opposed entering the Old City and taking what he called "all that Vatican," did not have any real religious education or understanding. He looked at events from what might, somewhat misleadingly, be called a purely "national" point of view. Like many others, he thought of the essential Jewish religious site in the Old City as the Kotel, and not the place of the *Beit HaMikdash*, the Temple Mount.

So instead of ensuring that the Jews would be able to pray on the Temple Mount, instead of making some compromise with the Muslims that would lead them at the hour of their weakness and defeat to recognize a Jewish place on the Temple Mount, Dayan did what no one – not even the Muslims – expected him to do. He handed the keys to the mosques to the Wakf. In other words, he left the exact same Muslim religious administration in place that existed before. And he thought – it turns out mistakenly – that by doing this, by waiving all Jewish rights, he would ensure a kind of peaceful relation between the Muslims and Jews.

Rabbi Goren, hearing what Dayan had done, was stunned. Rabbi Goren, who was deeply learned in everything connected with the Temple ritual, saw the liberation of Jerusalem in religious, redemptive terms. He no doubt pondered whether the Jews should begin to construct the *Beit HaMikdash* before the coming of the Messiah. But the very minimum he expected would be that Jews would be able to pray on the Temple Mount and have real control over it.

Dayan's action precluded such sharing from the outset, and it set up what in some ways, from the Israeli and Jewish point of view, is the worse situation of all. Israel is in effect in charge of the public order on the Mount, and so is the party to blame when there is any rioting or disorder. Jews have no religious rights on the Temple Mount at all, and if someone should ascend with a book of Psalms in hand, he would speedily be arrested. The Muslims have exclusive right to worship on the Mount, and yet are not content with the situation, and feel threatened by it.

Essentially the unfortunate and potentially tragic situation the Jews are in now in regard to the Temple Mount comes also because of the divide between the two great extremes of Israeli society: the secular and the religious. Dayan, the prominent representative of secular Israel was not concerned about Jewish worship on the Temple Mount. In subsequent years, Dayan would have been happy to have a Jordanian flag on the mosques and cede them to the Arab world. Along with him were many religious Jews, including leading rabbinic authorities, which was most surprising and painful for Rabbi Goren. The whole national aspect of the matter, the whole practical reality at hand was not of concern to these rabbis. They could not, and have not been able to, respond wisely to the remarkable change in the historical situation of the Jewish people, which occurred in 1967.

Rabbi Goren was a unique figure among the great, learned Jews of his time, in that he was deeply connected with the historical forging of the Jewish nation. In establishing the army rabbinate, in developing the *nusach achid*, in prayer, and in insisting on cancelling segregated religious units, he aimed to generate a greater unity in the people of Israel. Thus, as he understood it, the taking of the Temple Mount was significant for the whole of the people of Israel and had to involve a transformation in its religious life. So he made efforts, not only in the days immediately after the Six Day War but throughout the years, to return there to pray (if not on the Temple Mount exactly where he was prohibited, then in close proximity to it). But it should be noted and stressed that in all his work to reestablish Jewish worship on the Temple Mount after 1967, he did not write or make known to a wide public any design for impeding Muslim worship. In fact, the measurements he had made by army surveyors of the Temple Mount were made to ensure that Jews would not touch upon the prohibited areas where the Temple might have stood. It should be noted and stressed that in all his work to reestablish Jewish worship on the Temple Mount he did not once publicly advocate, and nothing in his writings contains any hint of, destroying or damaging the mosques. His whole demand for a place of prayer was in those areas to the south and north of the Mount, which had been added on to the expanse later, and which it was certain Jews could walk on without violating any religious prohibition. Because of all of this, Rabbi Goren's views and actions seem anything but irresponsibly extreme. Rather, they were courageous and responsible.

In his own writings on the subject of the mosques, Rabbi Goren repeatedly emphasized the point of the danger to Israel if any damage were done to the mosques. In addition, he was also concerned that, should the mosques be destroyed, Israel would then have the shameful task, from his point of view, of having to rebuild the mosques. But above all, he was tremendously wary of, and negative in regard to, any kind of action that would bring about a pan-Islamic "holy war" against Israel, which he assumed would immediately break out should the mosques be harmed.

Moreover, there is evidence prior to the Six Day War showing how Rabbi Goren was greatly concerned with protecting the holy places should Israel take them over. Months before the Six Day War, as part of his work in the chief army rabbinate, he had made detailed plans for protection of the holy places. He took this responsibility seriously, the responsibility of guaranteeing access of worship to people of all faiths. Regarding this, it should be remembered that one of Rabbi Goren's favorite verses he cited over and over again, is that Jerusalem should become a "place of worship for all peoples." His own religious vision was of all people flowing to the House of the Lord in Jerusalem.

Thus, when Rabbi Goren engaged in his famous struggle to build a synagogue on the Temple Mount, he carefully laid out the limited area on which such a place of worship could be built. As a religious Jew, he followed the rabbinic prohibition making the greatest part of the Temple Mount, including the area of the Mosque of Omar, off limits to Jews in an impure state, which is the accepted status of all Jews today. It makes little sense to think that Rabbi Goren would have wanted to destroy the mosque in order to leave the space blank and empty. Clearly there is no way he could have thought or ordered building the Temple by himself.

Thus, while it is impossible to prove conclusively and finally that Rabbi Goren did not ask Uzi Narkiss to blow up the mosques, it seems very unlikely that he made such a request. Such remarks are totally out of keeping with the position he publicly presented and fought for throughout his years as a public servant in Israel.

It is difficult to know how to challenge and destroy such a "fact of history" once it has been so widely disseminated. No doubt the analysis set forth here will not be able to erase what has by now become "common knowledge," which, in my opinion, is the result of politically motivated slander.

Hopefully, however, this discussion will bring some public awareness to how suspect and dubious this claim really is.

Chapter 38

WORSHIPING ON THE TEMPLE MOUNT: HOW NOT TO MAKE PEACE

One of the great disappointments in Rabbi Goren's life was his failure to establish a Jewish prayer presence on the Temple Mount. This was not for want of trying. Immediately after the Six Day War, Rabbi Goren conducted a service where he was certain was the permitted area of the Temple Mount for Jews according to halacha. He continued with this until he received a government order forbidding him to do so.

This did not lead him, however, to abandon his efforts. For years he came as close to the Temple Mount as he could, and prayed from the building Mahkameh, which adjoined the Temple Mount. Every year he conducted Yom Kippur services from this point overlooking the Temple Mount.

But all his efforts to rally the public and the government on this issue did not succeed. The fact that the overwhelming majority of rabbis ruled that it was forbidden to even walk anywhere on the Mount thwarted his efforts.

The combination of government wariness and what he saw as rabbinic timidity meant his dream of establishing a place of prayer on the Mount did not come to fruition.

Rabbi Goren responded to the dramatic change in the situation of the Jewish people in 1967 with a burning desire that the Jews also change, also move, if not to what was impossible, the Holy of Holies, then at least closer to it.

Ironically, perhaps Rabbi Goren's failure in attaining this objective also meant delaying of any real mutual recognition between Jews and Muslims. For by leaving the total religious control of the Temple Mount in the hands of the Wakf, Moshe Dayan in effect taught them that they need not recognize any Jewish rights on the Mount. This lack of recognizing Jewish rights on the Temple Mount appears to be obviously linked with the failure of the Muslim world to recognize Jewish rights to any part of the Land of Israel.

Rabbi Goren, had he succeeded, might have led gradually to a change in the Muslim position, a beginning of recognition of Jewish rights in the land and a beginning of a process of peace.

Chapter 39

LETTER TO THE GOVERNMENT: JEWISH PRAYER ON THE TEMPLE MOUNT

In a long letter he sent to the Ministerial Committee on the Holy Places, Rabbi Goren said he was shocked to the depth of his soul by the order to prohibit Jewish prayer on the Temple Mount. He wrote that this would mean that the Jews' holiest place, the place of the *Akeida* (binding of Isaac) and of the two Temples, the place to which all prayers by Jews are directed, is the single place in the land in which Jews would be forbidden to pray.

Rabbi Goren wrote that the Kotel can in no way be a substitute for the *Har* (Temple Mount), that the Kotel's holiness is a thousand times less. He wrote that the Kotel symbolizes the exile while the Temple Mount symbolizes the return of the people to its land and to its holy places.

He wrote that it must be clear that despite the "great theft" of the Muslims in building mosques on the sacred ground of the Temple, there is no intention of the Jews to in any way do injury to the Muslims' prayer on the Mount.

He added that there is not at present any halachic right of Jews to try and build a Third Temple, since this cannot be done until there arises in Israel a prophet who will have the right to do this.

He ended his letter with a plea to the ministers not to abandon the Jews' holiest place to the control of its desecrators.

The ministers did not, however, give an answer.

Chapter 40

RECOMMENDATION FOR JEWS TO GO UP TO THE TEMPLE MOUNT

Rabbi Goren devoted a great deal of time seeking to precisely determine the area of the Temple Mount upon which Jews were permitted to walk. He believed that by abstaining from visiting the Mount, the Jews were in effect ceding it to the Muslims.

He felt the Jewish claim to the Temple Mount was in danger. So he urged that Jews be allowed to go up as frequently as possible to those areas on the Temple Mount that Jewish law permitted.

Prior to going up to the Temple Mount the person must immerse in a mikveh for that purpose. This walking on the Temple Mount would be done without leather shoes.

As he understood it, going up to the Temple Mount was a *mitzva* that, in bringing the Jewish people together in their most holy place, brought them special protection. One of his disappointments was that more Jews did not regularly ascend the Mount.

He once said that just as it was permitted to enter the Holy of Holies to protect the Temple area, so it was permitted for Jews now to go up to the Mount in order to protect it.

Rabbi Goren was a relatively lonely figure in this approach, and his call was not heeded by the great mass of the people. To this day the Temple Mount tends to be neglected by most of the Jewish people.

Here, indifference, and perhaps cowardice, combine with rabbinical prohibition. There is a strange alliance between the political left who would cede the whole area to Muslim control and religious leaders, who seem to have abondoned their responsibility for shaping the Jewish future.

Chapter 41

A WARNING TO MENACHEM BEGIN

In 1982, as Prime Minister Begin was about to set out to Camp David to negotiate with Anwar Sadat, rumors circulated about intended Israeli concessions on the Temple Mount. The whole right wing of Israeli politics was in turmoil and those most concerned about the issue selected Rabbi Goren as their representative. Rabbi Goren, concerned already about the absence of *de facto* control of the religious places, was nonetheless troubled at the thought that Israel might officially concede sovereignty to a foreign power. He went and spoke with Begin and received his assurance that Israel would make no sacrifice of sovereignty on the Temple Mount. Despite the tremendous pressure placed on him at Camp David, including from within his own delegation, Prime Minister Begin did not yield on this issue.

Chapter 42

HISTORICAL PRECEDENT FOR PRAYER ON THE TEMPLE MOUNT

According to Rabbi Goren, Jews had had a synagogue on the Temple Mount from the time of the Muslim conquest. At that time, the Jews were responsible for setting up, lighting, and cleaning up the candles.

They were later forced to leave the area near where the mosque, the Dome of the Rock, had been built. But according to Rabbi Goren, they continued to pray there. Still later, when forced away from there, they prayed in the building called the Mahkameh, where Rabbi Goren himself prayed for many years on Yom Kippur. This building adjoins the Temple Mount, without being on it.

There is the question of how the Jews prayed on the Mount when there was the prohibition of *tumat met* (ritual impurity resulting from contact with the dead). One supposition, though, is that they went in accordance with the opinion that the destruction of the Temple cancels out the whole matter and consequent application of *tumat met*.

In any case, Rabbi Goren felt there was long historical precedent for a Jewish place of prayer on the Temple Mount, since it wasn't the *Beit HaMikdash* itself. In the special survey he had conducted after the Six Day War, the results of which appear in his work on the Temple Mount, he went through great pains to find out, measure and calculate exactly the area where it is halachically permitted to walk.

THE DIASPORA AND THE SHOAH

Chapter 43

DIASPORA COMMUNITIES AND ALIYA

For Rabbi Goren, the creation of the State of Israel meant that there could no longer be justification for Jews remaining in their communities outside of the Israel. For him, *aliya* was not reserved for those who were forced to come as refugees, it was the religious obligation of each and every Jew. Frequently he clashed with leaders of Disapora communities who did not like hearing his frank, unambiguous message on the subject.

For Rabbi Goren, the total ingathering of the exiles was one of the signs of the Messianic age. It was also the fulfillment of the Divine promise to the people of Israel.

Thus, those who had the opportunity to come to live in and help build the Land of Israel, and did not take this opportunity, were failing not only themselves, but the Jewish people as a whole.

This sense of the central meaning of *aliya* was a lifelong conviction of his. The Shoah of the Jews of Europe only intensified this conviction.

Chapter 44

A Trip to Poland

The journalist Shlomo Nakdimon, in an article in *Yediot Ahronot* published on May 25, 1984, described Rabbi Goren's four-day trip through Poland. He begins his account with a picture of Rabbi Goren standing in the cemetery of a small town, his lips muttering prayers, and tears flowing from his eyes. In this town, as were so many others in Poland which had once thrived with Jews, the only Jews left were in the cemetery.

Rabbi Goren had to wait twelve years, according to Nakdimon, until he was given permission to visit Poland. In the meantime, Rabbi Goren had worked with Rabbi Arthur Schneir in New York to help establish the International Organization to Preserve Jewish Burial Places in Poland. In March of 1984, Rabbi Goren arrived in Poland, accompanied by Yosef and Frieda Shorer, wealthy Jews who were to fund preservation work at the cemetaries. Rabbi Goren wished to visit the graves of his maternal parents in his city of birth, Zambrow, and that of his father's family in Warsaw.

The trip as a whole was filled with painful disappointments. Rabbi Goren, who had left Poland at the age of six, still had memories of the Jewish life there. But now he returned to almost nothing. Rabbi Goren also visited the death camps of Maidenek and Treblinka and read out memorial prayers there. Yosef Shorer inquired of an elderly neighbor in his hometown about the fate of the Jews, including his parents. He learned that they had not been taken away to the death camps, that rather they had been forced from their homes, a huge pit had been dug, and they had been shot to death there. Rabbi Goren did not succeed in locating the graves of his grandparents in Zambrow. Since some of his family were Gerrer hassidim, Rabbi Goren sought out the graves of the Sfat Emet and the Chiddushei HaRim in Gur. He did not find them – as in so many other places the Nazis had smashed the graves and used the stones.

Rabbi Goren was asked whether seeing these things did not destroy his faith. He answered as follows: "According to the Rambam, man is capable of free choice. He can be as evil as Yeraboam ben Navat or as righteous as Moshe Rabbeinu. If there is no freedom of choice, then there is no place for reward and punishment. This is true for individuals and also for nations.

"The Jew was created in order to provide a test for the behavior of the nations towards him. The Shoah was the most horrible test of the world. There, except for the Danes, no nation stood the test.

"It is said, 'You are to be a chosen people from all the nations.' It is forced upon us to be the test for the behavior of the other nations. Should the Allies have sent a few bomber planes to Auschwitz, in which there was no air defense, it would have been possible to hit the death camps and to give masses of prisoners their opportunity to escape and be saved. But no nation other than the Danes stood the test." (Quoted from Shmuel Nakdimon's May 25, 1984 article in *Yediot Ahronot*, with my translation.)

Chapter 45

LESSONS OF THE SHOAH

For Rabbi Goren, the Shoah was not only the most horrible historical instance of man's inhumanity to man, it was proof that the barriers that mankind had supposedly erected against great evil had in no way stood the test. Rabbi Goren indicated that the collaboration of the Vatican with the Nazi criminals was one serious proof that religion alone provided no secure defense against evil. So too, the great scientific and technological progress of mankind, which many had hoped would translate into progress in the moral life of mankind, also failed. It was the most cultured and enlightened nation of Europe that proved to be the most barbarous. Moreover, modern technological means facilitated the destruction, and multiplied the evil.

The barrier that Socialism and a world of equality and brotherhood supplied, also amounted to nothing. The great percentage of the nations and people of the world stood idly by, and a very great percentage contributed to the evil. The dream that mankind would, in its modern phase of development, show real caring also did not stand up.

The lessons of this for Rabbi Goren were clear. The Jews must never again allow themselves to be dependent upon others for their security and personal safety. Nations that Jews had seemed totally at home in, and had contributed greatly to, turned overnight against them. So, however good life in the Diaspora communities might seem in the present, life for Jews in them was not secure. It was impossible for the Jews to rely on any people other than themselves. They had to learn to defend themselves. The State of Israel was to be not only the homeland of the Jews who lived in it, but the defender of the Jewish people wherever they were.

As Rabbi Goren saw it, *Eretz Yisrael*, the State of Israel, was the only real place of refuge for the Jews. The building of Israel and the creation of a third *malchut* (kingdom) was to give all the Jews a home they could be secure in.

ETHICAL TEACHINGS

Chapter 46

Baseless Hatred and Gratuitous Love

Rabbi Goren maintained that the Torah teaches that all hatred, which is not in accordance with the mitzvot of the Torah, and is on a purely personal basis between individuals, is forbidden and considered a form of baseless hatred. There is, however, hatred that is based on a *mitzva*, such as the hatred one might have to one who is in open and conscious violation of the Torah, and commits *chillul Hashem*. This hatred is not simply permitted, but required.

Nonetheless, considering the great destruction baseless hatred has brought in the world, even according to the Sages, including being responsible for having brought about the destruction of the Second Temple, Rabbi Goren sought out the remedy for this most prevalent form of hatred. And he finds it in the *Yerushalmi*. For there it is taught that the only true remedy to such hatred is gratuitous love.

It is in the loving of one's neighbor as one self, in the constantly seeking to practice the *mitzva* of loving the other that one is able to resist and overcome the impulses to hatred that are natural to us. The Torah, according to Rabbi Goren, gives us a path to overcoming self-destructive baseless hatred through seeking to judge everyone favorably.

It is this attitude and example which was clearly demonstrated by Rabbi Goren in his unending efforts to do *chesed* for others.

Chapter 47

FOUNDATION OF RABBI GOREN'S THOUGHT: "AS GOD IS MERCIFUL AND COMPASSIONATE, SO ARE WE TO BE MERCIFUL AND COMPASSIONATE"

In a number of Rabbi Goren's most well-known and controversial rulings, he seemed to be guided by the rule that the halacha is given so that Jews may be able to *live* by it. In other words, he sought to find a way within the halacha to meet the human and Jewish needs of those who petitioned him. This was not a matter of going outside the halacha, which he would in no case agree to do. It was, however, a matter of being guided in halachic decisions by a principle of compassion and concern for the human being.

As God is merciful and compassionate, so are we to be merciful and compassionate. Both in his halachic rulings and in his actions as chief army rabbi, Rabbi Goren's compassion and concern for the individual human being was apparent time and time again. He took upon himself controversial cases for which he was certain to receive public scorn (such as the Langer case), if only to help needy individuals. He went out of his way to make halachic rulings (such as in allowing the *agunot* of the sailors of the two lost Israeli ships, the *Dakar* and the *Eilat*, to remarry) that helped individuals build new lives. He showed courage and dedication to the well-being of soldiers in seeking ways to enable them to fulfill their religious duties while simultaneously doing their job as soldiers.

He not only helped, but did so when considerable personal risk and sacrifice in time and investment were required. Because he helped so many is one reason many people had such strong positive feelings about him.

Chapter 48

Work Ethic

Though Rabbi Goren was no doubt endowed with an extraordinary mind and a memory far beyond the ordinary, both his prowess in Torah and his success in so many other areas of life would not have been possible had he not been so tremendously dedicated to his work.

Already as a very young man he was dedicated to learning. At Hebron Yeshiva he was always the first to open the yeshiva in the morning and the last one to leave it at night. His son, Rami, estimates that this dedication in learning enabled him to go through the whole of the *Shas* over one hundred times in his lifetime, and to go over certain especially complicated and difficult Talmudic tractates, such as *Yevamot,* over 250 times. It is well known that when he was the chief army rabbi he would precede the morning prayers with learning, and then immediately afterwards return to learning. Throughout the day, wherever he was going, he was always learning; he acquired much Torah learning in the journeys between various army bases.

But his great dedication was present not only in learning. He was the kind of person who gave total devotion to whatever he did. When he was involved as army chaplain, he showed no letup in work. He was endlessly on the go visiting the soldiers and helping them out. So too, in giving responses to the thousands of halachic inquiries that he received. He worked and worked long, long hours, slept little, and moved on to still more work.

This energy, conviction, and devotion no doubt came out of a sense of his fervent belief that he was doing sacred work. His energy came out of the conviction that as a servant of God he must do his duty in the most complete way possible.

Here, however, there is of course a question of priorities in work, and whether or not he was always wise in what he devoted himself to. There are people who felt he would have been more wise had he taken less time to care for communal needs, and given more time to his research and writing in Torah.

Chapter 49

Extraordinary Pains to Help Others

The enormous effort and care Rabbi Goren would take in order to help people was something all his close associates experienced. Once he learned about a person's problem, and decided to help, he did not spare any effort to assist.

In contrast to his gruff exterior, Rabbi Goren was an extraordinarily warm and kind human being. Time and again he showed a surprising thoughtfulness toward others.

His longtime assistant, Aryeh Shumer, related the story of Rabbi Goren's first encounter with the Langer problem. He told how Rabbi Goren, despite many pressures and pressing problems, gave hours of his time to the frightened eighteen-year-old soldier telling the family story.

At the height of great historical moments, Rabbi Goren would time and again turn to the needs of individual soldiers and families

The *chesed* he displayed in risking his life to bring to proper burial many fallen soldiers, whose families would otherwise have been tormented, was very great. So was the whole enterprise of teaching and learning Torah in the army, enabling so many to have religious knowledge and experience that they otherwise would have missed.

Once Rabbi Goren had in mind to help someone, he did not stop until he achieved the task. Even in acts of *chesed*, his strength of character and determination were of greatest value.

Chapter 50

TO SAVE ONE SOUL IN ISRAEL

Rabbi Shear Yashuv Cohen, Chief Rabbi of Haifa and brother-in-law of Rabbi Goren, said that Rabbi Goren dedicated himself many times to saving a single soul in Israel. When this involved risk of his own position, and considerable public criticism, his family would ask him, "Why should you become involved and risk bringing down such condemnation upon yourself?" His answer would invariably be, that to save one soul – to rescue a soul – for the congregation of Israel, was a deep historical and religious obligation. He would say that if it is possible to save a Jew, it must be done. Rabbi Cohen said that Rabbi Goren saved many many souls in Israel who would otherwise have been lost to the Jewish people.

FAMILY AND FRIENDS

Chapter 51

RABBI GOREN AS A FATHER

One of the most difficult challenges for a public person is not to be so swept up by responsibilities to the broader community as to neglect home and family. All through the years of his married life, Rabbi Goren was a tremendously busy person. But this did not prevent him from being a deeply loving and caring father. He was close to all three of his children, and each one of them has repeatedly expressed a tremendous respect, admiration, and love for him.

Because he could not be at home for holidays when he needed to serve his soldiers, he most often brought his family to celebrations at army bases all over the country

Rabbi Goren often took his son, Avraham (Rami), with him on his travels to visit soldiers in all parts of Israel. He often conditioned these visits on his son's learning a chapter of the *Mishna* by heart. For the young boy growing up, these trips were a great adventure. For Rabbi Goren, they were opportunities to be with his son and educate him.

Rami Goren has said that though his father loved and was devoted to Torah above all and was a great genius in this area, he did not pressure his son to give his life wholly to Torah. Rather, Rami Goren has said that his father cared above all for the well-being of the children and did not try to make use of them to serve his own agenda. Warm and loving, yet demanding in terms of respectful and moral action toward others, Rabbi Goren did not suppress his children's initiative and independence. Rather, he tried to encourage and support them in their chosen paths.

His trust and closeness with his children extended through their adult years, when he could consult with them and make use of their advice. On one such occasion, when he was about to leave the Chief Rabbinate's office, and start a new political party, the firm "no vote" of his children and wife was decisive. He developed friendly and close relations with his childrens' spouses, who also became part of the extended Goren family. Through the years of his illness, after his three heart attacks, it was his son-in-law, Dr. Israel Tamri, who attentively supervised his care.

His son Rami helped him in many ways, including with the publication of his works.

All the children describe the special joy of holidays with their father, his singing and liveliness, and the warmth of his humor.

Their great respect and love for their father is an indication of the warmth and love he showed to them.

Chapter 52

Rabbanit Tzvia Goren

There is a saying that ninety percent of a man's happiness in life depends upon his choice of wife. There is no doubt that Rabbi Goren was especially blessed in this ninety percent, and in marrying, found the perfect companion to aid him in his life of service to the people and God of Israel. Tzophea (Tzvia) Cohen was the daughter of one of the outstanding religious personalities of the *yishuv*. Her father, the *nazir*, was a close associate of Rav Kook. Her brother, Shear Yashuv Cohen became the Chief Rabbi of Haifa.

A student of Hebrew University when she and Shlomo Goren first met, she was not simply highly intelligent, but could understand the special burden that comes with living with a person of special distinction, upon whom are made almost unending public demands.

The Rabbanit recognized her husband's brilliance, and from early on was dedicated to helping him achieve his life's aims. She was not only a loving, devoted wife, but was his champion, who identified with and shared his life goals. Most importantly, she gave him the stable loving family he so needed.

In their first years of marriage, Rabbi Goren's father, a widower, lived with the young couple. Later, the children came; first Droria (born on Pesach), then Tehiya, and then Avraham (named after Rabbi Goren's father). Each brought a special happiness to the home.

The Rabbanit might, in a sense, be said to have sacrificed something of her own professional advancement in order to be totally ready to help Rabbi Goren when he needed it. But for her this was no sacrifice, as she saw in him the much more important personality, the one the people of Israel truly needed.

For close to fifty years she gave him the home and support that enabled him to give so much to the Jewish world.

For Rabbi Goren, family loyalty was a cardinal value. The Goren's total dedication to and faith in each other is reflected in the united family front the Goren children and their families presented, both when Rabbi Goren was alive, and in the years after, when together they were devoted to consecrating his memory.

Chapter 53

FRIENDS AND ASSOCIATES

In a certain sense, Rabbi Goren was a loner, one who spent long hours in study by himself, one who clearly struck out on his own individual path. But in the course of his life he had a long list of friends and associates, *chavruta*s, and comrades in arms.

Rabbi Goren's closest friend, according to his son Rami, was the Jerusalem religious court judge (*dayan*) Rav Eliezer Shapira. The two had learned together in their youth at the Hebron Yeshiva. According to Rami Goren, the two spent hours together on the phone discussing passages in Torah. They would joke with each other, ridicule each other, and above all learn with each other. One of the few times Rabbi Goren ever cried in his life was when he heard that his old *chavrusa* had passed from the world.

Another close associate of Rabbi Goren was Rabbi Yitzhak Alfassi, his successor at the Goren family shul, Kommemiyut Avraham. The synagogue had been founded by Rabbi Goren and named after his father. Rabbi Alfassi, who is the author of many books on *hassidism*, was in a sense a *hassid* of Rabbi Goren. For years they *davened* and learned together. Rabbi Alfassi was a fervent disciple of Rabbi Goren, and his great knowledge and sense of humor were for years a source of help to Rabbi Goren.

Rabbi Goren's closest assistant in the army for many years was Rabbi Menachem HaCohen. The climax of this friendship was their experience together during the Six Day War. Though they were to move apart politically, the friendship between the Goren and HaCohen families continues to this day.

In his long career and through many difficult tasks, Rabbi Goren had a very large number of friends and associates. I regret that I do not know them all, and probably will miss many of the most important while mentioning just a few friends here.

One close associate was the *gabbai* of Kommemiyut Avraham for forty years, Mordechai Flint. HaRav Moshe Klein, Dov Kopito, HaRav Micha HaLevi, and HaRav Yisrael Ariel are some others.

There is also a long list of army rabbis who served with and under Rabbi Goren, whose devotion to him was great. A number of his drivers, Aryeh Shalom for one, were especially close to Rabbi Goren and served with him for many years. Among the journalists who were his friends, was the one who accompanied him in the 1967 entrance into the Old City, Yossi Ronen. Rav Goren promised to officiate at Ronen's wedding, which he later did. Another long-time journalist friend was Shlomo Nakdimon. All these people, and many others, knew the special loyalty Rabbi Goren's intense idealism and energetic service of Israel inspired.

Chapter 54

RELATIONSHIP WITH YITZHAK RABIN

Rabbi Goren and Yitzhak Rabin served together in the Israeli Army for over twenty years. They were friends whose families attended each other's family celebrations. They shared many difficult moments, and also the great moments of victory, as in the Six Day War. There, Rabin was one of the true architects of the victory, while Rabbi Goren had an important and inspiring part, especially in all that was connected with the reclaiming of the holy places and the Old City of Jerusalem. Rabbi Goren had great respect for Yitzhak Rabin because of his great personal honesty and fairness. Rabbi Goren trusted Rabin more than any other Israeli political leader, all of whom he knew well.

Toward the end of his life, Rabbi Goren was both surprised and disappointed by the part Rabin had in the Oslo agreement. How, he asked, could the person who had spent his life fighting for Israel, give in to a bunch of terrorists and agree to arm them and give them part of *Eretz Yisrael.*

Nonetheless, despite the disappointment, the friendship between the Goren and Rabin families continued.

When Rabbi Goren died, he was mourned by then-Prime Minister Rabin as a decisive figure in the creation of the military rabbinate, as one always present in places of danger to strengthen the fighting soldiers, and as one who made an important contribution to the building of the State of Israel.

CHARACTER AND REPUTATION

Chapter 55

COURAGE AND GENIUS

Rabbi Goren had a quality that even his worst enemies would never deny that he had: extraordinary courage. This courage first manifested itself when he was a small child fending off Arab intruders, and going miles by himself through hostile territory to gather food for his impoverished family. It was evident in the countless times in which he risked his life and inspired his fellow soldiers in battle. It was evident in his daring to take risks that no one else dared, whether in going behind enemy lines to retrieve the bodies of fallen soldiers, or exposing himself to enemy fire in charging ahead of the fighting soldiers. Rabbi Goren was renowned for his great personal courage. When asked about this once, in his apparent fearlessness he replied, "I always like to be with the soldiers. I never was afraid. During the War of Attrition, I would pray each morning on the *rampot* (ramps) along the Suez Canal. They shot and they shot, and nothing happened to me. Once, one of the positions collapsed, and two soldiers were trapped within. I went to get them out. They said to me that it was very dangerous. I received permission and I went and lay in that place for seven hours, digging the sand away with my hands, burrowing my way in until I reached the bodies and brought them out. In those seven hours, the Egyptians did not bombard the position. The moment I got out of there, a tremendous shelling began. I did not for one second believe that I am a *kadosh*, a holy person, but I do believe I have Divine Providence watching over me."

His courage was also evident in his willingness to make courageous halachic decisions, though this sometimes won him only the hostility and boycott of powerful religious groups. His courage was also manifest in confronting the most powerful military and political figures in Israel of his time, and standing for the right as he saw it.

His courage was in going to extraordinary pains, even extremes and risks to his own reputation, in order to help worthy individuals in need. And it was also, sadly, present when he dared to defy leaders and influential friends who he had worked with for years when they did what was, in his eyes, wrong for the State and people of Israel. His courage was in his ability to fight for the right in every way possible, with all of his being, with an intensity and wholeness that are rare in this world.

Along with his courage was his extraordinary power of mind, his genius in Torah learning and in mastery of religious thought. This genius was perhaps most manifest in his work as *posek*, where he showed the capacity to learn and master the most complicated subjects in all their technical detail. It was also apparent in his incredible memory, grasp of the sources, and in his ability to formulate a coherent and meaningful Jewish religious philosophy. This genius, which made him, in the eyes of those who opposed him, one of the *gedolei hador*, one of the true Torah greats, was achieved and maintained despite the need to give the greatest amount of his time to practical rabbinic duties.

Taken together, his courage and his genius make him a most extraordinary personality in modern Jewish history.

Chapter 56

CONVICTION AND TIRELESS ENERGY

It is perhaps difficult for many living in Israel or throughout the Jewish world to understand one key to Rabbi Goren's special strength: intense conviction. In a world where hesitation and doubt and intellectual uncertainty play such a large role, Rabbi Goren seems, in a way, old-fashioned and out-of-style. For while he was second to none in his capacity to understand philosophical arguments and questionings of his opponents; he was nonetheless, first and foremost a person fueled by tremendous energy and belief in the rightness of his way of seeing the world.

He was a person of conviction who believed with all his heart that he knew the right way for *Am Yisrael.* This conviction explains in part his great leadership capacity. He did not flounder over the right way. He knew the right way and was willing to direct others toward it.

This, combined with his tremendous energy, enabled him to do so much in bringing about the realization of his own vision.

Chapter 57

LOYALTY

Aside from his courage, genius, energy, and enterprise, Rabbi Goren had
other admirable character traits. He was a person of great loyalty, both to
his ideals and to the people to whom he was close. Loyalty to each one
with whom he had been truly connected characterized him all his life.

It meant that he held on to what became unpopular positions, and
fought for them when others who had long been identified with them
abandoned them. On the personal, level Rabbi Goren had no respect for
those who were moved to infidelity. His reluctance to officiate at the
second marriages of divorced people is perhaps an indication of how
much importance he placed on maintaining personal loyalty, even in
difficult relationships.

Chapter 58

TREMENDOUS POWER OF DETERMINATION

All through his life, Rabbi Goren displayed a tremendous power of determination, an extraordinary capacity not to be deterred by obstacles and to realize his goal. His strong will, even in the face of opposition from those in more powerful positions than he, was evidenced time and time again in his life. Consider the way he confronted Ben-Gurion and all the other major leaders he knew. This will and determination, this conviction that he was right, was displayed both in thought and in action. Once he decided to do something, he did it, whether that was learning a new subject in a completely thorough way, or risking his life in a minefield to bring to *kever Yisrael* the remains of soldiers.

It may be that his own great brilliance, which became apparent so early, strengthened his will. He was widely recognized as an *ilui* (gifted Talmudic genius) at a very early age. Of course his brilliance was connected with his great capacity to sit and learn for days on end, a capacity he also displayed very early.

But there can be little doubt that his ironclad faith in his own judgment was central to this power of determination in action.

The question of why this power was so strong in him must, to a degree, remain a mystery. One can speak of his parents, especially his mother, as having been strong and determined, but this cannot be the whole of the explanation. Clearly there is some element in it of a Divine gift.

This power of determination, this decisiveness, this faith in his own decision, was critical in his being a leader, and critical to his work as *posek*, as one rendering halachic verdicts.

Chapter 59

As Leader

Rabbi Shear Yashuv Cohen, in speaking of Rabbi Goren as an outstanding leader of his generation, said that the test of the leader is not when all is going well and is quiet. The test of the leader is when there is great trouble and difficulty, when there is a great storm and the boat is shaky in the waters. According to him, Rabbi Goren proved his leadership in the most turbulent and difficult of conditions. He did not hesitate to go out ahead of the rest at great risk to himself. He dared to confront great leaders, most notably Ben-Gurion, and stand on principle against them. He pioneered and took on halachic problems, questions that no one else was ready to answer. He learned completely new areas of Torah in order to be able to respond with knowledge and wisdom to new halachic problems. He did not waver in fighting for what he believed in, and he did not bow down or cower before any human being, however great in position and power.

He also put his own life on the line time and again to serve the people of Israel. As a leader he went first, went out ahead of the rest. He dared where no one else dared, and he did this with boldness, conviction, and strength. He gathered around him, especially when he was Chief Rabbi of the army, a group of strong and devoted supporters. He set an example for them by his always doing first what he expected others to follow and do. He demanded much of them, but always demanded most of himself.

Chapter 60

CONSISTENCY IN LIFE AND THOUGHT

Rabbi Goren is remarkably consistent in his attitudes and opinions. His sense, for instance, of the centrality of the Land of Israel is in his thought from the beginning, and continues through all of it. His fundamental outlook on life was set at a relatively early age, and he never really deviated from it.

Consistency was also central in his human relations. Once he had decided for you, he was for you wholly. Consistency in this sense connects up with loyalty. His love for and dedication to those he loved was absolute, and this was especially so in regard to his wife and children.

Chapter 61

ABSENCE OF REGRET

Toward the very end of his life, when he was burdened with illness and was deeply disappointed by the direction the Oslo agreement had taken Israel, he was asked if he had major regrets about his life. His answer was a resounding no, and a declaration that he had always done what he had to do. He did not regret or take back anything, and did not express sorrow at how he spent his life.

Nonetheless, if there was one area in which a voice of regret might have been heard from Rabbi Goren in regard to his life, it is in the area of learning and the Torah he might have given the world. He estimated that had he not been so involved in public service in the army, he would have written much more including a new scholarly edition of the *Yerushalmi Talmud*.

Chapter 62

Price of Being a Leader

Throughout his life, Rabbi Goren was subjected to strong opposition from very strong people. He contended with the major leaders of Israel in his struggle to deepen religious life in the state. But, worse, he was also subjected to bitter personal attacks and insults, and even slander from whole communities. This situation became especially acute at the time he was Chief Rabbi. His ruling on the Langer case turned broad sections of the hareidi community against him. His dispute with Rav Ovadia turned much of the Sephardi world against him. The secular Left, long suspicious of him, was repelled by his devotion to the greater Land of Israel. There were also those repelled by his personal manner – his apparent arrogance and gruffness.

These voices of opposition often turned to slander and personal abuse. More than once, false rumors were spread against him, for instance in regard to the question of his going abroad to have heart surgery.

In a sense he was no different from anyone who takes a strong position, fights for an ideological stand, and thus can expect to have many opponents. But because of his eminent position and the many worlds on which he had influence, the opposition was great and varied.

Chapter 63

A MAN OF CONTROVERSY

Throughout his public life, Rabbi Goren was at the center of controversy. He was frequently attacked, and even hated. The number of his critics at certain points of his life seemed to outnumber those of his passionate supporters.

No doubt part of the reason for this related to Rabbi Goren's directness of speech and thought. This *"sabra"* (native Israeli) gruffness, this giving no sympathy to nonsense, and speaking one's truth as directly and forcefully as possible, characterized him throughout his life.

This directness, forcefulness, and belief in his being right were connected with the fact of his singular brilliance, his being a person of such vast knowledge and learning. This sense of his own understanding, so much more than others, may have made him at times impatient with those slower in mind and apprehension. There was perhaps some trace of arrogance.

Thus it might be suggested that, in some cases anyway, a bit of diplomatic skill or of a certain kind of politeness in listening to others, might have been helpful to him. He did not put up with fools gladly, even when these fools were people of high reputation and authority.

Still this constant embroilment in controversy is also evidence of more positive characteristics. Rabbi Goren was a person who cared immensely for the Jewish people, Israel, the Israeli Army, and individual soldiers. He was a person of immense love and kindness.

His outer harshness was connected, as all those who knew him can firmly attest, with an inner kindness and softness. He would be fierce in struggling to do justice for those he regarded as having been wronged. His impatience related to his love of justice and concern for the well-being of others. It was a humane impatience. And it was impatience most often in the service of something outside of Rabbi Goren himself. He was willing to alienate half the rabbinic establishment if it meant helping a brother and sister that otherwise would not have been able to marry.

He was willing to defy the most venerated minister of Israel of the time – Moshe Dayan – after the Six Day War on the matter of prayer on *Har HaBayit* and the Cave of the Patriarchs, which he regarded as of supreme significance to the Jewish people.

We see from this how much he was a person who took responsibility. He was a person who did not leave it to others, but would always do the job himself. If we speak today of the threat to Israeli society that comes from those who are *rosh katan* (small minded) we can better appreciate him, for he was the very opposite of an avoider of responsibilities. Time and again he ran in to do the job, often risking his life where others would not. In a place where there was no one else, he was the one who acted. He certainly fulfilled the saying from *Pirkei Avot*, "Where there are no men, strive to be one."

He was someone who passionately put forth his own views, and who fought for them. In a sense he was a soldier all his life, a fighter all his life, and this spirit of competitiveness played into most of his human encounters and dealings. In a strange way, it also had its source in that world of learning to which he was so dedicated all his life. There are countless stories of how he would contend and argue with his long-term partners in learning, how he loved the give and take of this kind of intellectual and spiritual struggle.

His tough mind and character were part of his integrity, but they too were unavoidably responsible for his making enemies, including those who once had been his friends. Criticism of him became especially acute in Rabbi Goren's later years. It was a source of great pain to him. For after all, one of his paramount teachings was of the love for all of *Am Yisrael*. He worked all through his life for the unity of *Am Yisrael*.

Chapter 64

Shortcomings

There is no perfect person. The person closest to God, Moshe, was denied entry into the Promised Land because of a moment of disobedience and loss of faith. All the heroes of *Tanach*, great and small, are presented truthfully, with failings revealed.

With these examples in mind, it is possible to consider what appear to be Rabbi Goren's shortcomings. Despite – and perhaps to a degree even *because* of – all his extraordinary abilities and virtues, there were unnecessary conflicts with others and errors in action and judgment.

From an early age, Rabbi Goren was recognized as having special talents and abilities. His courage and decisiveness evidenced an extraordinarily strong character.

No doubt in part because of these abilities, he had great confidence in his own judgment and rightness. The negative side of this is that he did not always have tolerance and patience with those whose abilities were less than his and whose views differed from his.

This meant that he often offended people who might have, with a softer and more indirect approach, been brought closer to his own opinion. He occasionally, and unintentionally, insulted others who wished to present a different view to him. He was not always the best listener to those who had a different way of seeing things than he did. It was difficult for him to see and admit an error on his part. All of this shows a weakness in his ability to persuade, where the failure to show minimal understanding and sympathy to the position of the other can be taken as crassness and insensitivity.

Another of Rabbi Goren's shortcomings was his love of public glory and adulation. However well-deserved the accolades and recognition he received in his lifetime, there were instances in which he seemed to go overboard. For example, he staged a reclimbing of Sinai after the Six Day War, where there was a strong feeling that what was being done made little sense religiously. Another had to do with the controversy over the Agam sculpture.

His honesty, his directness, his firm belief in his own opinion, and also perhaps the yeshiva training in which so much energy is given to argumentation, resulted in that Rabbi Goren was often involved in controversy. Most of these, as in his struggles with Ben-Gurion and Dayan for proper religious behavior in the army, were clearly for the sake of Heaven. But the number of his public quarrels over time was so great that quarrelsomeness came to be seen as a central element of his character.

Rabbi Goren characteristically avoided a quiet, behind-the-scenes *darchei noam* approach to disputes. He spoke openly and honestly about what bothered him, and this led to his being continually involved in confrontations.

As Chief Rabbi, some of his most famous disputes were with the Sephardi Chief Rabbi Ovadia Yosef. Without going into the particulars of the disputes, it is fair to say that the very fact that there were public disputes did harm to the Chief Rabbinate and to the reputation of the Chief Rabbis. This happened because the public as a whole was looking for harmony and cooperation between the rabbis, as well as for the Ashkenazi and Sephardi communities and *Am Yisrael* as a whole.

Rabbi Goren's kind of imperial style, which suited the army's Chief Rabbi, was not the correct one in the Chief Rabbinate. In other words, Rabbi Goren did not show flexibility in approach, which might have improved the public image of the Chief Rabbinate.

Rabbi Goren was a man of truth on all accounts. One major reason friends and family urged him not to enter the political fray was that they sensed he did not have the capacity for acting, or the capacity for fudging the truth, which is often required in political life. He did not know how to restrain himself, and not say what he felt and believed to be true. He did not know how to woo a public with flattery, how to soften criticisms when he felt them.

This also perhaps explains why he was not able to translate the enormous popularity and prestige he had as Chief Rabbi of the army into a more successful Chief Rabbinate of Israel.

Around the holiday of *Shavuot* of 1967, Rabbi Goren conducted a ceremony on Jebel Musa in Sinai, which to many seemed superflous and self-aggrandizing. His heroics in the taking of the Kotel and the Temple Mount, and in the Cave of Machpelah in Hebron were genuine historical events. The ceremony he conduced on Jebel Musa seemed to many to be a ridiculous show without any real historical meaning and content. However, Rabbi Goren felt the action was connected with having entered a redemptive era. In any case, this operation did not win him friends, and allowed many critics to say that instead of serving the national interest he was here serving only his own ego.

One image of the pioneer generation of Israelis is of tough, hard people fighting each other for the "little" that there was. This was in every area of life. They were hard, stubborn, persistent unyielding people.

Rabbi Goren fits this picture in many ways. He lived through periods of real hunger and starvation in childhood. He knew what it was to struggle intensively to reap and work the land and to fight for the little it gives.

He therefore found it difficult to be generous toward rivals and he found it difficult to forgive someone who opposed him. This was especially true in regard to the public battles he had as candidate for the Chief Rabbinate of Tel Aviv as well as for the Chief Rabbinate of Israel.

One of Rabbi Goren's failings was his inability to recognize and help any successor of his. This was true regarding his successor for chief army rabbi, and also became true in regard to the position as Chief Rabbi in the Chief Rabbinate, especially when Rabbi Lau took over this post. It was as if Rabbi Goren so identified himself with each position (and this is truly understandable regarding the Chief Rabbi of the army post, since he essentially created it) that he could not imagine it going on without him. The criticism he made of Rabbi Piron during the Yom Kippur War, and the interviews he gave chastizing Rabbi Lau for not having the credentials in learning to be Chief Rabbi, did not help Rabbi Goren. Rather, they diminished his standing in the eyes of many.

The record would seem to indicate that Rabbi Goren had a difficult time recognizing the value of, and giving credit to, others involved in the same activity as he. This would seem to be borne out by the fact that he did not develop the kind of following which might have been expected from a person with his talents. On the other hand, many of his associates and subordinates showed a fierce loyalty to Rabbi Goren, and tell of his showing special consideration for them.

Chapter 65

MISCONCEPTIONS GATHERED AROUND RABBI GOREN

It is fair to say that Rabbi Goren suffered much in his life because of public misunderstanding of his actual thought and practice. These misunderstandings were, at times, deliberately magnified by those who wished him ill.

Perhaps the most egregious misunderstanding related to Rabbi Goren's character was that he was regarded by a certain part of the public as inhumane and indifferent to the sufferings of others because of his decisiveness and great confidence, and perhaps also because of his very firm views on military matters. Yet his whole career is filled with examples of the opposite of this, of acts of extraordinary kindness made often at great risk to himself and great personal sacrifice.

He was regarded as being indifferent to the well-being of non-Jews, despite his placing great emphasis on the idea that in Messianic days there would be a flowing of all people to the house of the Lord in Jerusalem. Moreover, he had close ties with the *Noahide* groups in Israel, whose members he tried to help. He also cultivated friendships with those he believed to be true supporters of Israel when he visited foreign countries.

Some of the worst slander of Rabbi Goren came from the ultra-Orthodox community in the wake of the Langer case. As he himself belonged to this community their attacks on him were a source of particular anguish.

Another set of slander came when Rabbi Goren suffered a heart attack. At the time, there was only one physician, Daniel Gur, who was capable of doing bypass surgery in Israel. As the Goren family prepared to have this surgery done, Dr. Gur told Rabbi Goren's son-in-law, Dr. Israel Tamri, that he could not possibly operate "under the eyes of the whole nation." He then recommended that Rabbi Goren go abroad to be operated on.

This story, however, appeared in the popular press in a different form. There, it was stated that Rabbi Goren insisted on being operated on abroad, that he was wasting the taxpayers' money in doing so, and what is most important, that he, the alleged advocate and lover of *Eretz Yisrael*, was proving hypocritical.

This story caused Rabbi Goren and his whole family considerable embarrassment. It was only upon Rabbi Goren's return from the operation that Dr. Israel Tamri, after speaking with him, induced Dr. Gur to explain the whole incident to the newspaper. Dr. Gur did so, admitting that it was only because of his refusal to operate and his recommendation for the operation to be done abroad that it had been done in this way. But of course, the retraction could not completely erase the damage that had been done to the Goren name.

Another source of slander against Rabbi Goren came over the whole controversy with Rabbi Ovadia. Here, a whole rumor mill was created to almost daily undermine Rabbi Goren's authority and reputation. As a person of truth, Rabbi Goren could not fight back by making a rumor mill of his own. So in this rivalry he suffered from having to be on the defensive most of the time.

Another great source of hostility came from his opponents on the political Left, and their many supporters in the media. Rabbi Goren was attacked by the Israeli Left, who called him a narrow chauvinist and a warmonger. The effort to attack and undermine his personal reputation was primarily to undermine the whole *"Eretz Yisrael HaShleima"* camp. The accusation was that Rabbi Goren was against peace and that his attitude and position prevented the kind of compromise that would have brought true peace to the area. Here again, there was a failure to understand the true character of Rabbi Goren's position. For him, there was no question of his own personal view on the matter, but rather of the halachic status of *Eretz Yisrael*. In discussing the question of "land for peace," Rabbi Goren dealt with this in terms of what he understood the halacha to be on this, rather than in terms of his own personal preference. One proof of this was when Rabbi Goren was asked about the Golan Heights' halachic status as part of *Eretz Yisrael*. In this matter, he gave an answer that infuriated those who most strongly identified with him. As a man of truth, he simply stated the halachic position that the Golan is not within the halachic boundaries of Israel. He did not say this because he wanted to surrender the Golan Heights, but rather because this was the position of the halacha. Again he was subjected to personal attack when people accused him of bowing to the political will of his friend, Yitzhak Rabin. But again, the question was not politics or personal preference, but ruling in accordance with halacha.

RABBI GOREN AS *POSEK*

Chapter 66

OUTLOOK AS A *POSEK*

Rabbi Goren made it clear more than once that one should do everything possible in making a halachic ruling in order to help the concerned individual. He would always proudly say that he was from Beit Hillel. However, he always made it clear that in no case could this mean violating the halacha. These two principles were at the basis of many of his rulings. At times, he would go against a majority of *poskim* of the past and would at times make rulings that seemed to some non-conventional, but he would never permit himself to go outside of halacha to do this. For instance, when asked about women's army service, he said he could not possibly rule in favor of this as all *gedolei Yisrael* had spoken against it.

Yet he was always looking for ways to help and improve the situation of others. Rabbi Goren shared the basic Jewish view of technological innovations that mankind is put on earth to help complete the creation and that these innovations are not something to be feared or rejected out of hand, but rather to make wise use of. All that is given by God can be used by God's creatures to make a better world.

Chapter 67

RABBI DR. ABRAHAM STEINBERG ON RABBI GOREN AS *POSEK*

Rabbi Dr. Abraham Steinberg, one of the world's most distinguished experts on Jewish medical ethics, has long attested to the distinctiveness of Rabbi Goren as a *posek*. Dr. Steinberg, in an evening devoted to Rabbi Goren's memory at Kommemiyut Avraham synagogue in November 2001, spoke about Rabbi Goren's daring and innovativeness. He spoke about Rabbi Goren's willingness to deal with complicated and controversial issues. He spoke about the deep knowledge and thorough research that Rabbi Goren gave to problems in medical ethics. Steinberg spoke about a special blend of six qualities that made Rabbi Goren great as a *posek*. According to Dr. Steinberg:

1. he was an *ilui* in Torah;
2. he had up-to-date knowledge of the latest developments in all areas of life;
3. he had the power to clearly and decisively decide;
4. he had an eagerness to tackle all problems, and was not deterred by either the complexity or the controversial character of the problem;
5. he had an ability to not simply make a decision, but to make sure it was put into effect, and
6. he had the feeling of the present's urgent demands and would not simply relate to and rely on what was important in the past.

These qualities taken together, said Dr. Steinberg, defined Rabbi Goren as a pioneering figure in the world of halacha. He was without question the most important figure in all that relates to providing religious soldiers a halachic guide for proper army service. He was one of the pioneers in rulings on problems of medical ethics raised by new technological developments.

There is no doubt, according to Dr. Steinberg, that Rabbi Goren was a most humane *posek*, who sought a halachic way to answer human need, especially when it came to painful human problems, such as that of the *agunot*.

Rabbi Goren saw himself as, and always acted in his own mind, within the framework of halacha. In his work as a *posek*, he was seeking a human answer within an objective framework of knowledge. In this, as in all else, he was guided by *yirat Shamayim*, an awe and respect before the Almighty that made his work, as he saw it, not that of a creator in modern terms, but rather as a servant of God in traditional terms.

Chapter 68

WELL-KNOWN HALACHIC RULINGS

Rabbi Goren essentially wrote the book on military halacha. He is the one who first responded to questions soldiers in the field asked on all areas of their lives.

The Agunot Rulings

When it became apparent to Rabbi Goren that there was no hope of finding alive the Israeli Navy personnel who had been lost with the mysterious sinking of the *Dakar* and the *Eilat*, he ruled that the *agunot* of these sailors could remarry. This was one of the many instances in which Rabbi Goren in his role as *posek* ruled in a way that took into deepest consideration the human needs involved in the situation.

Hallel on Independence Day

Rabbi Goren ruled that *Hallel* should be said on the evening and the day of *Yom HaAtzmaut*. This question of *Hallel* is to this day controversial and confused in Israel, where the same shul can have a number of different minyanim, each with its own *minhag*. But Rabbi Goren's ruling reflected his sense that a dramatic transformation in Jewish history required a change in our action so as to show recognition of the blessing we have been given and correspondent gratitude to God.

The Doctor's Strike Ruling

Rabbi Goren was deeply troubled by an unprecedented and, for most of the public, shocking doctor's strike in 1983 that took place after a prolonged wages dispute. He wrote then, that it is forbidden for doctors to strike hospitals and outpatient clinics when this might endanger human life. He spoke about the positive obligation in halacha to restore a lost object (i.e., the bodily health of the person) and the negative obligation not to cause unnecessary suffering and pain.

However, he also ruled that doctors have the right to demand from the state the wages they earn and that the state was obliged to pay these wages.

On Ransoming Captives for an Excessive Price

Despite the great value placed in the Jewish tradition on rescuing captives, Rabbi Goren ruled that we do not rescue prisoners for an excessive price, basing himself on a *mishna* in *Gittin* that states "for the good order of the world."

On Whether the Besieged Fighters at Masada were Justified in Taking their Own Lives

Rabbi Goren ruled that they were justified in taking their own lives, since their capture would have led to their violating fundamental prohibitions of the Torah. He argued that their capture would also have led to the desecration of the people of Israel because it would have given the enemy something to boast about. He referred to the example of King Saul as a precedent.

On the Burial of Non-Jewish Soldiers

Lev Pisachov, a non-Jewish soldier serving in the Israeli Army, was killed by the Hamas near Tulkarm. He was interred outside the gate of the cemetery in Beit Shean. Then-Defense Minister Yitzhak Rabin ordered that his body be brought into the military cemetery and buried alongside his Jewish comrades. When asked about this, Rabbi Goren, citing Rabbi

Yoel Sirkes, the Bach, said that when Jews and gentiles die together, they can be buried together. Rabbi Goren said he had made many such rulings during the time of his tenure as chief army rabbi. He was outraged that it was Jews who do not serve in the army who insisted on this separation. Rabbi Goren said the act of burying separately is a desecration of God's name.

Firsts in Medical Law

Rabbi Goren was the first rabbi to permit the transplantation of organs in Israel for the purpose of saving human lives. He was a staunch proponent of donating limbs for organ transplant, despite the strong cultural bias against this practice. He was also the first to rule that in vitro fertilization, artificial insemination, could be used in select cases.

The Lev Kipnis Case

Lev Kipnis was a fifty-two-year-old new immigrant from Russia who was killed in a motor accident. Doctors could not identify him at first and could not reach his relatives to ask permission to use his organs for transplants. They used the organs for transplants anyway, to the objection of a number of hareidi experts and secular philosophers. Rabbi Goren, when asked, said that the *mitzva* of saving life comes before all, and that therefore the doctors were obliged to take the organs, even if they did not ask permission. He said that this case was not a matter of religious controversy.

Chapter 69

CASE OF THE BROTHER AND SISTER: THE LANGER CASE

Perhaps the most famous and controversial domestic halachic dispute the State of Israel has yet known is what is commonly called "the case of the brother and sister," or "the Langer case." This case stirred the nation in the period before Rabbi Goren was elected Chief Rabbi. One of the great expectations of the wider public when he entered office was that he would provide a solution to this case. He did, but at the expense of making some important, unforgiving enemies.

The case centered on the matter of *mamzerut* and of the prohibition of a Jew marrying someone with this legal status. The Langers were two young soldiers, a brother and a sister serving in the Israeli Army. They were both engaged to be married. They were the children of a woman born into the *hassidut* of Rimanov who had met a non-Jew named Bolek Borokovski, in Poland. Her parents had insisted that this man convert to Judaism before their marriage. He had agreed to do so, but there was a real doubt as to the validity of his conversion. Whether the brother and sister would be able to marry depended on the validity of the conversion.

After separating (not divorcing) from Borokovski, the woman, who would later be the mother of the two Langer children, married again in Israel. Yehoshua Langer was the father of the two young soldiers in question. If her first marriage was a valid Jewish one, this meant that her second one was invalid and the Langer children were *mamzerim,*

The case was taken to a religious court in Petach Tikva, which tried to determine whether Borokovski was, in fact, Jewish. He was invited to the court and tried to affirm his Jewishness, but there was much contradictory evidence. He knew, for instance, that a Jew puts on *tefillin* in the morning, but he did not know how to do this. He could not complete the first sentence of the Shema. Nonetheless, the court ruled that he was Jewish, thus ruling that the brother and sister were *mamzerim*.

Rabbi Goren met the Langer brother and sister when they were in deep psychological distress. He also met them at a time when the country was very much stirred up by the case. Both Prime Minister Golda Meir and Defense Minister Dayan were eager for the status of *mamzerut* to be lifted.

Rabbi Goren's way of dealing with the problem was controversial. He convened a special rabbinic court. He also did something extremely unusual, he allowed all the other judges to retain their anonymity. He did this, of course, to prevent them from coming under threat of attack.

Rabbi Goren considered the Jewish historical relation to *mamzerut* and as Shear Yashuv Cohen has written, he knew that many of the great Sages of Israel had made special efforts to keep people from the status of *mamzerut*.

After carefully checking all the evidence that could be found about Borokovski, including claims that he regularly ate pork and attended a church, Rabbi Goren ruled that his conversion was not valid. This meant that the Langers's mother's marriage to Yehoshua Langer was her first halachic marriage. This meant that her children were not *mamzerim* and they could marry in a regular Jewish ceremony. The very day of the ruling, Rabbi Goren saw to it that arrangements were made for the long-delayed marriages of the two young people to their respective partners to take place immediately.

Rabbi Goren was attacked in an unprecedented way for this ruling. The claim was that he had given in to political pressures and had violated halacha in order to satisfy the demands of the secular elite. The whole human dimension of the case was totally ignored by those who began a vile, abusive campaign against him. This attack, abuse, and hatred came early in Rabbi Goren's service as Chief Rabbi and cast a shadow over it throughout.

Chapter 70

INTERVIEW WITH RABBI JOSEPH KLAUSNER

Shalom Freedman (SF): Can you outline Rabbi Goren's general position and standing as a *posek* today?

Rabbi Joseph Klausner:[*] If you mean sociologically, then different groups have different relationships to him. If you are referring to how the permanent evaluation of Jewish history and halachic thought will accept him, I have a definite position. Sociologically, those groups that liked and accepted his Religious Zionism and advocated what he advocated obviously looked up to him. Unfortunately those groups that were not sympathetic to his approach and for whom he was not their leader, looked to the side in reference to him. But it is not only Rav Goren that they were against. The extreme hareidim were also against people like Rav Kook and Rav Soloveitchik *ztz"l*, and any groups that represented the institutions of the State or the Zionist transformation of the Jewish people. This was especially true in his case because he came from the yeshiva world and was actually hassidic, and they knew that he was a great rabbi. Indeed, at the age of seventeen he was well known to Rav Isser Zalman Meltzer and Rav Kook, *ztz"l*, and they both wrote the highest of praises of him in letters. Thus, the hareidim knew he was great, but because he was so great and was not part of their *derech*, there were groups that did more

---

[*] Rabbi Dr. Joseph C. Klausner received his Ph.D. from Yeshiva University for work on Rambam's Mishne Torah, and received rabbinical ordination from Rav J.B. Soloveitchik. His vast knowledge is especially pronounced in all that is connected with the historical development of Religious Zionism. He lives in Israel where he learns and teaches Torah.

than just attack him – they tried to ignore him. However, from a historical perspective I think that he will be considered very important. Since he didn't just deal with *mutar* (permitted) or *assur* (prohibited), *patur* (not obligated) or *chayav* (obligated) to perform a certain action, he dealt with how to deal with new issues from a new perspective. He wanted to deal with contemporary issues. He was unique in that he didn't see the halachic process as divorced from what you would call *machshava* (philosophical thought) or even *Kabbala*. He could quote a *Zohar*, Maharal, and other sources with a *Minchas Chinuch* or *Avnei Nezer* – two sources he liked – and reach a halachic decision.

SF: In what areas did he provide new rulings?

Rabbi Klausner: While he was Chief Rabbi of the army, and while he was Chief Rabbi of the State of Israel, the focus of his public halachic ruling was obviously on those *halachot* that have to do with public Jewish life: what do you do in the army on Shabbat, for example; also moral questions that had to do with the army. In 1981–3, there was a famous dispute for the sake of Heaven with Rav Israeli, *ztz"l*, about how the conquest of Beirut should be achieved. Do you leave a *petach patu'ach* or do you not leave a *petach patu'ach*? He dealt with issues that had not been seriously raised for close to 2,000 years from the time of Yehoshua; from the days of the First Temple.

On the public level, he dealt with all issues, for instance how we celebrate *Yom HaAtzmaut* properly. Even though Rav Goren was young, the veteran Rabbinical leader HaRav Yehuda Leib HaCohen Maimon relied on him. For Rabbi Goren, *Yom HaAtzmaut* is no less a holiday – maybe more – than Purim or Chanuka. It is like the kind of holidays that were instituted by the rabbis, and he gave it a flavor, a mold. He was very forceful in regard to saying *Hallel* with a *bracha* on *Yom HaAtzmaut*. This was the way he dealt with the public *halachot*.

But he also dealt with those private *halachot* that were important, like the *psak din* (ruling) in the case of the Langer brother and sister. There were other local issues that he dealt with. For example, a person living outside of Israel coming to Israel for the three Pilgrimage Festivals. Does he keep a second day of *Yom Tov* or not? For Rabbi Goren, it wasn't just a matter of looking at the issue from a technical point of view, i.e., asking questions like "Do you have an apartment in Israel?" "Are you dependent on your parents?" or "Are you a yeshiva student?" Rather, it was essential to look in broader terms, such as where is the person "holding" in relation to living in *Eretz Yisrael* and appreciating the life in *Eretz Yisrael*.

There is now a third level that is starting to come out, at least from the new volume I have seen, *Trumat HaGoren*. Rav Goren was asked questions that are halachic, but also more research-type questions; questions for the twentieth, and obviously now for the twenty-first, century. For example, Rabbi Goren dealt with the question of wearing a *kippah*. Wearing a *kippah*, if you ask a *posek* of his generation, is obvious. But if you go back five hundred or a thousand years, the *poskim* have different opinions. Rabbi Goren tried to bridge the gap between the generations and deal with the issues. I think this is very important. He dealt with the research and came down with a relevant conclusion for the time.

SF: Who are the principal halachic authorities he relied on? My sense is that the Rambam was his preferred source?

Rabbi Klausner: Rav Goren published a book on the *Yerushalmi*, and the way he understood the *Yerushalmi* is the way he felt the Rambam understood the *Yerushalmi*. Now in reference to *Geula* (the Redemption), there is a dispute between Rambam and the *Yerushalmi*, and Rav Goren felt the preference had to go to the earlier source, the *Yerushalmi*. Nevertheless, the Rambam and the G"Ra, I would say, were his two main influences throughout the ages because they do not have a limited halachic frame of reference, but rather have a large scope. It's also other commentators of the *Talmud* and Rav Saadia Gaon, to a certain degree, who influenced him, though we do not have much halacha from Rav Saadia Gaon. In Rabbi Goren's book on the *Chagim*, he brings rulings from Rav Saadia Gaon and also from the Kuzari. But he also brings the regular halachic sources, such as the Maharam of Rottenberg. He liked the Chatam Sofer, who was an *ish halacha* but with a broad base, and was relevant to Rabbi Goren's generation. The Chatam Sofer fought the Reform movement and Rabbi Goren tried to fight the secularists. Obviously, Rav Kook was his model in reference to how you create a halachic framework in a new Jewish civilization, in a new Jewish State of Israel. He liked the *Avnei Nezer* because he came from the same type of Polish background. He was also aware of the academic research – one could even call it critical or scientific research – that was done. He did not always quote it, but he was totally aware of what was being done academically. You can see an example of it in his book on the *Yerushalmi*, the *Yerushalmi HaMeforash*. He was clearly aware of it. If he wanted to quote it openly, that's another issue. Maybe he thought that it would hamper acceptance of some of his books.

The Rambam was not just a source, but a decisive factor in his thinking. If there was a Rambam that went against someone else's ruling, he would rely on the Rambam, or Rav Kook.

SF: Do you know the story of Rabbi Goren's composition of the *Yerushalmi* and the question of what he did or did not do on it?

Rabbi Klausner: I can tell you what I know, though I am sure it is not complete. I've heard things here or there. From Rav Goren I heard that there are twenty-four volumes on the *Yerushalmi*. I cannot say whether it was all written, whether it was edited, or whether it was something he had in his mind. But he said that it was going to be twenty-four volumes of *Yerushalmi*, and it was going to be major. He mentioned this. I asked him about this once when we were talking about some of Rav Kook's writing. We spoke in 1984–85 when they were marking Rav Kook's fiftieth *yahrtzeit*. There was a conference at Bar-Ilan University. On the way back, we spoke. He had mentioned Rav Kook's book, *Moreh HaNevuchim HaSheini (The Second Guide to the Perplexed)*. He talked about it at other times as well.

Some say his *Yerushalmi* exists. Some say it does not exist. It hasn't come out yet. We spoke about Rav Kook's writings. He told me that he had a lot of ideas, but he needed time to put them out. In the 1990s, a few years after Rav Goren's demise, Bar-Ilan's Talmud department, headed by Professor Z.A. Steinfeld, held a *Yom Iyun*; their annual Talmudic conclave, and it was dedicated to Rabbi Goren's writings. It was publicly understood that part of what Bar-Ilan received – the rights and material of Rabbi Goren's *Yerushalmi* – came through Rabbi Shear Yashuv Cohen. They spoke about his *Yerushalmi* coming out. But, unfortunately, nothing came out of it. (Subsequently, I have heard that there was no material given to Bar-Ilan. One version is that there was no material to give to Bar-Ilan. Another version I heard was that it got lost in Bar-Ilan. Another was that the family could not locate it.)

Rabbi Goren published five chapters of his *Yerushalmi*. Maybe he intended to develop this. He had many articles published.

SF: Rabbi Goren is seen by some people as externally rough and uncaring. Yet it seems to me that, halachically, he took great care to rule in a humane way. Is there a concept of a "humane halachist" and would it apply to Rabbi Goren?

Rabbi Klausner: There's a term that is used by a lot of *ba'alei halacha*. They refer to *poskim* that are *yir'ei halacha*. Rabbi Goren was not *yor'ei halacha*. In other words, there are some halachic persons that will tell you privately, "I would like to say so and so, but if the majority of *rabbanim* don't agree, I can't do it." In other words, we can't try to find a *heter* here because it goes against the mainstream. Rabbi Goren said what he felt. He was a *takif behalacha*. In other words, it didn't matter if all the *rabbanim* thought one way, and all the politicians thought another way, he said what he thought. "*Lo tagur mipnei ish*." He said what he thought. And when you say what you think and you want to get things accomplished, sometimes you offend others. He came in and built up the Chief Rabbinate in the army and gave it the character that it should have for the whole community. He felt that religious Jews shouldn't have to fight for their kosher kitchen or their little *shtiebel*. Rather, the whole army should be made kosher. So when you want to do that, you have to fight. In his generation, you had a lot of very strong people in the army. He would argue with Moshe Dayan and then say, "Let's go to Ben-Gurion." He told me this many times.

Once, when *Yom HaAtzmaut* was supposed to be on Shabbat or on Friday, he went to Dayan and wanted to push it forward. Later he changed his halachic ruling and said that it was too bad that his old ruling was valid. He felt *Yom HaAtzmaut* had to be kept as a halachic day on its original date.

It's known he was a tough person. He did not want to deal with the lower echelons. He was close to many politicians, yet could also break with them. For example, Yitzhak Rafael was the one who helped get him elected as Chief Rabbi. But later he split with him because he did not like what he was doing with conversion. Only in the 1990s, after he retired as Chief Rabbi, was there a rapprochement and Dr. Rafeal, head of the Mossad HaRav Kook, recommended him for the "Maimon Prize." In the end, he gave the prize money back because he said that by this time he had enough money. He was very polite, but more important for him was the truth. On the subject of the Golan, he had an opinion that put him out of favor with a lot of his supporters. But he stated his opinion anyway. Whenever he had an opinion, he stated it.

I have heard Rabbi Louis Bernstein, *ztz"l*, speak about Rabbi Goren. He thought that the two greatest *rabbanim* and *poskim* of this generation were HaRav J.B. Halevi Soloveitchik and Rabbi Goren. With Rav Soloveitchik, people could accept or not accept him, but it wasn't a personal thing. With Rabbi Goren, there were a lot of personality questions involved. He was very *takif* (forceful) and could readily alienate people.

On the other hand, there were many people I saw (including "*amcha*," the common people) who loved him. A number of Torah scrolls that were dedicated to Rabbi Goren were dedicated by Sephardim or Yemenites, real *amcha*, because what he tried to do in the army was to unite Jews of all backgrounds. This was the purpose of his introducing the *nusach achid*, the uniform prayer liturgy for all.

For HaRav Goren, there was no Ashkenazi or Sephardi, or this level or that level; halacha was for everyone. He was opposed to the idea that the Ashkenazim represent the higher standards of halacha. Halacha was for all of *klal Yisrael*. Therefore, he was opposed to the idea of a *Badatz* that was good only for a limited few.

SF: The fact is that he built the Chief Rabbinate of the army, but with all the expectations, there was disappointment in what he did as Chief Rabbi of Israel. He was portrayed by the secular media as divisive.

Rabbi Klausner: I would say the following. If one would talk to the educated layman Israeli who lived through Rabbi Goren's period, if you would ask him who were the Chief Rabbis of Israel, he would know two, maybe three, names: Rav Kook, Rabbi Goren, maybe Rav Lau (*sheyibadel lechayim tovim ve'aruchim*). But Rabbi Goren will be remembered as a major Chief Rabbi. He wasn't just a Chief Rabbi who was at ceremonies. He wasn't just a Chief Rabbi for the religious. Even if people didn't agree with him, they felt his presence. They knew he cared for the Land of Israel. I think everybody knew that he was in the army in 1967. I think that the secular Israelis respected Rabbi Goren. Shlomo Lahat said that he and Rabbi Goren disagreed about every issue. But there was one rabbi that the secular Israeli considered to be a real rabbi; it was Rabbi Goren, not Rav Shapira after him and not Rav Unterman before him, even though both are known as great halachists. He was the Chief Rabbi of all Israelis. He wasn't the rabbi of the *Mizrachi* or the Religious Zionists. He was the *Israeli* Chief Rabbi. He was a Religious Zionist, but he came in as himself. This was so much a part of his power. "He wasn't just a rabbi of the army," as someone said when he died, "he was the *Aluf* (General) among the Rabbis, and the Rabbi among the generals."

He was a paratrooper. He could have been a high-ranking army person, even if he wasn't in the Chief Rabbinate.

I think that Rabbi Goren was the first Israeli, totally Israeli, Chief Rabbi. He was not like Rabbi Ovadia who represents an ethnic group. He spoke the language of the Israeli society. He knew the beat of the society.

SF: You mentioned Religious Zionism. Do you think that Rabbi Goren would use those words in relation to himself?

Rabbi Klausner: He didn't want to be part of the *Mizrachi* apparatus, but religious Zionism was his place. He was not close to the Agudah even though he knew the *rabbanim*. He had studied in the Hebron Yeshiva. Many of those who later became the Agudah *rabbanim* were his friends. But it was very clear to him that he was a Religious Zionist. He was a Modern Orthodox Religious Zionist. But he set his standards, not others.

SF: In his halachic rulings he set the standards and went into areas where others would not go.

Rabbi Klausner: In medical issues, with the submarine *Dakar*, in quasi-halachic issues, in moral issues, he set the standard. The thing that he lacked was a real yeshiva of his own. He had a little something with the Idra Yeshiva, but he did not have anything like Mercaz HaRav. I think what he would have liked to have been was the head of a major yeshiva.

But Rav Shapira has the yeshiva (Mercaz HaRav) and so the eighteen-year-olds, the young boys, identify with Rav Shapira (shlita). He has the multitudes. Rabbi Goren did not have the attention of the multitudes because he did not have a major yeshiva behind him. His shul in Tel Aviv was a nice shul, but he did not have a movement. He had thought about setting up a political party in consultation with Rav Ovadia Yosef (shlita), but Rav Ovadia set up a party (*Shas*) himself.

SF: He advised Rav Ovadia Yosef on politics. They became allies again when they were both fighting for the approval of their third term as Chief Rabbis of Israel.

Rabbi Klausner: He officiated at the wedding of Rabbi Ovadia Yosef's daughter. He was *mesader kedushin* for a few of Rav Ovadia Yosef's grandchildren. And almost every year Rav Ovadia comes to the *azkara* (memorial service) for Rav Goren.

Rav Goren represented the total *hashkafa* of what the hareidi camp could not accept. He wasn't just different; he was the opposite of them. He had come out of their world and they knew he was great; but he was different.

So the only thing that they could try to do was to ignore him. For instance, in a book about Rav Isser Zalman Meltzer, the authors do not quote *rabbanim* who were not their style. Rav Goren does not appear at all in the book, even though he was one of the people who were close to Rav Isser Zalman Meltzer.

Rav Shach, the noted Ponivetz Rosh HaYeshiva, asked Rav Goren to set up a *kollel* with him in 1960 when the Brisker Rav passed away. Rav Shach had been in Yeshivat HaDarom in Rehovot for a period, and he wanted to be in the Pardes Chana area. One of his ideas was to set up a *kollel* and the person he thought would be best suited to work with him was Rav Goren, though they did not have the same worldview. They had known each other through Rav Isser Zalman Meltzer. Both respected the Brisker learning. Rabbi Goren was in the army, and thus was not interested in building a *kollel* at the time. Rav Schach never attacked Rav Goren.

SF: Did he have *talmidim chaverim* (student-colleagues)?

Rabbi Klausner: Pinchas Peli (a Jerusalemite who was close to Rav Soloveitchik) was close to Rabbi Goren. On Friday nights, when Rav Goren was in Jerusalem, he used to learn with a group of people. At one point, Rav Shear Yashuv Cohen was in that group. He respected Rav Goren tremendously. To this day, Rav Shear Yashuv is the one who continues to perpetuate Rav Goren's legacy.

By the way, I'll add to a question we spoke about before. If there was one rabbi that Rabbi Goren identified with and wanted to be seen as the pupil of, it was Rav Kook.

He made sure that he would be buried next to Rav Kook's grave. That's his place in history. He is the *talmid muvhak* (the outstanding pupil) of Rav Kook in his generation. No one else holds that distinction. He saw himself as the continuer of the *derech* of Rav Kook.

SF: He learned with Rav Kook from the time he was a child of ten.

Rabbi Klausner: When he was seventeen, he walked into the room and Rav Isser Zalman Meltzer stood up for him. The only similar story I heard was that the Chofetz Chaim stood up for Rav Meir Shapira of the *Daf Yomi* when Meir Shapira was thirty-eight. The Chofetz Chaim said, "I cannot sit down until Rav Meir, the Lubliner Rav, sits down." This was the same show of respect by Rav Meltzer for Rav Goren.

In 1947–48, Rav Goren had discussions with the *Eida HaHareidit* about digging on Shabbat. He had no problem telling *rabbanim* that they did not know halacha. The one person that tried to keep Rav Kook's *derech* in the army was Rav Goren. He was very Israeli, like most Israelis of the time.

The *talmidim* of Rav Shaul Israeli (Rosh Yeshivat Merkaz HaRav and member of the Chief Rabbinate) say that two things broke Rav Goren and Rav Shaul Israeli. One was Oslo. The second was Rav Ovadia's position on Oslo. Both of them had been close with Rav Ovadia for many years.

SF: Isn't it true that when we hear of Rabbi Goren today, it is mostly in connection with halacha?

Rabbi Klausner: Not necessarily. He is always represented as one of the strong rabbis on *Eretz Yisrael* from the perspective of Religious Zionism. In other words, if you have to name the six great Religious Zionist rabbis, it would be Rav Kook, Rav Zvi Yehuda Kook, Rav Neriya, and Rav Goren, followed by those the young folks would put in today, Rav Shapira and Rav Eliyahu. Rav Goren was the *rav* of all Israel. Rav Goren had status. Even his opponents knew that he was big. He liked and he lived off of controversy. He was a fighter. He wanted to do things. He didn't just sit back and talk. He acted and labored for *Achdut Yisrael* (the unity of Israel). Rav Goren was for *Achdut Yisrael*, but he didn't just talk about it. He acted. In this, he was the greatest.

WRITINGS

Chapter 71

METHOD OF RABBI GOREN'S THOUGHT

Whenever Rabbi Goren addressed a subject, he addressed it as a Torah scholar. He did not ever work off the top of his head. Rather, his way of thought was first and foremost a way of study. He gathered the sources and read them together, interweaving them in the world of his own assertions. Point by point in any argument he was backed up by sources. The presentation of his own views often took the form of a reading out of the views he had gathered.

A great part of his thought – perhaps the greatest – consisted of his halachic rulings. These always involved him in a rigorous scholarly method, which aimed at considering the issues on all sides. It meant detailed involvement with the small practical details of everyday life. This, too, marks one of Rabbi Goren's unusual strengths, that unlike many other thinkers he did have a great capacity for dealing with the small practical details.

Another feature of Rabbi's Goren thought is the vast range of subjects he tackled. He was ready to go into controversial areas where others were afraid to tread. It is possible to have some idea of the range of his thought by looking at a small sample of the issues and questions he addressed.

1. The status of the governing authority in Israel according to the halacha
2. The sanctity of the Land and *pikuach nefesh*, i.e., the saving of life according to the halacha

3. The halachic status of Judea, Samaria, and Gaza
4. The love of Israel and senseless hatred
5. The question of who is a Jew in the eye of the generations
6. Freedom of choice and religious coercion
7. Taking the census in accordance with halacha
8. The origins and halachic status of Ethiopian Jews
9. The building of Jerusalem and the ingathering of exiles toward the third period of redemption
10. Determining the poverty line according to halacha
11. Freeing prisoners in exchange for terrorists
12. The State of Israel according to the vision of prophecy and halacha
13. The Messianic age
14. Halacha and the people's will
15. The halachic status of Jerusalem Day
16. Whether Torah scholars enhance peace
17. The religious significance of Independence Day
18. The State of Israel according to the halacha and prophetic vision
19. The sanctity of man and the holiness of the Land
20. Jewish prayer on the Temple Mount
21. Requirements for conversion
22. A Jewish peace plan
23. The Holy Land and the value of life
24. Whether the Torah was given on Shavuot
25. The attempt to rebuild the temple sixty years after its destruction
26. Are we still living in the period of the Exile?
27. Reasons for atonement

Chapter 72

WRITINGS

Through the years of his service to the people of Israel, both the army years and the years in the Chief Rabbinate, and subsequently, Rabbi Goren persisted in learning and scholarship. He told Rabbi Alfassi that he had forty volumes in preparation, only a few of which came to light during his life. After he left the world, his family began the publication of his writings, under the supervision of Rabbanit Goren and Avraham Goren. To date, over ten works of his have appeared.

Rabbi Goren's first book was *Nezer HaKodesh*, which appeared in 1935 when he was only seventeen years of age. The work received endorsements from Rav Kook and Rabbi Isser Zalman Meltzer. The book was written as a series of lessons (*shiurim*) on the Rambam in a style common to the *yeshivot* of the time. It is distinguished by the acuity of its *pilpul*.

His second book was *Sha'arei Taharah*, which is on *masechet Mikvaot*. The book is a kind of *Talmud Bavli* to the *mishnayot* on this tractate. Its citations are taken from all the sources of Oral Torah, including the work of the *Rishonim* and *Acharonim*. The work contains a commentary based on the *pshat* (straightforward meaning) of the Torah and the Rashi commentary.

Rabbi Goren's great dream was to bring out a new revised edition of the *Jerusalem Talmud*. This project occupied him for many years, but he finished only a small part of it. The first part of this included eight chapters on *masechet Brachot*. Rabbi Goren won the Israel Prize in the category of Torah scholarship, in 1961, for this composition.

A comprehensive article by Rabbi Goren entitled "Vilna Gaon and the Jerusalem Talmud" was included in a large work compiled by Rabbi Yehudah Leib Maimon. This article became the basis of a lifetime of research on the notes that the Vilna Gaon made on the *Jerusalem Talmud*, and led to the publication of Rabbi Goren's work, *The Vilna Gaon and the Jerusalem Talmud*.

Rabbi Goren's work, *The Sabbath and the Festivals*, was worked on during his years in the rabbinate. It includes his pioneering view of how to celebrate *Yom HaAtzmaut*, Jerusalem Day, and reflects on the State of Israel as a stage in the vision of redemption. The work contains an exposition of the traditional view of the holidays as given in halacha, *Agadda*, and in Jewish thought.

Three of Rabbi Goren's works are: *Torat HaMoadim*, *Torah HaShabbat and HaMoed*, and *Moedei Yisrael*. The purpose of these works, according to Rabbi Goren, was to unravel the sources – the historical, philosophical, and mystical roots – of the holidays.

Rabbi Goren began to collect his various halachic rulings in the volume *Meishiv Milchama*. Three volumes of this work contain his responses to questions on almost every aspect of military life. They are pioneering volumes in an area where the rabbi stands above others as halachic authority. They reflect his long army experience, his role in founding the IDF Chief Rabbinate, and being the first rabbi of the Israeli Army.

The fourth volume of the work *Meishiv Milchama* has its own special status. It is the most comprehensive work done on the whole subject of the Temple Mount. It contains up-to-date mapping of the Mount, based on special surveys Rabbi Goren ordered. It contains a comprehensive introduction, including commentary on great events of recent history in which the rabbi himself was involved. It contains documents of historical value on a great variety of subjects, such as the orders given to safeguard the holy places given before the Six Day War. It asks questions such as, "Who will build the third *Beit HaMikdash – Am Yisrael* or *Melech HaMashiach*?" It contains Rabbi Goren's historical account of the events that led to the denying of Jewish access to the Temple Mount. This work is the most comprehensive work on this subject by a *gadol* of Israel. This work, according to Rabbi Shear Yashuv Cohen, is a kind of will and testament from Rabbi Goren to the political leaders of Israel. He sent a copy to them when he was on his deathbed, as they were engaged in negotiations with the kingdom of Jordan that might have taken *Har HaBayit* out of the hands of Israel. Rabbi Cohen says that in his final visit to Rabbi Goren, he spoke about this book, about a letter he sent to the negotiators. He wrote about how pained Rabbi Goren was when discussing this subject.

In the posthumously published volume, *Torah HaMedina* (a halachic and historical research on those subjects that stand on the agenda of the State of Israel since its founding), there is an exposition of Rabbi Goren's political philosophy and thought.

Among the subjects of the work are:

- The *aliya* of our father Abraham to *Eretz Yisrael*
- The sanctity of land and the saving of life in accordance with halacha
- The authority of the *Sanhedrin* and that of the men of the Great Assembly
- The electoral system according to halacha
- The territorial integrity of *Eretz Yisrael* according to halacha
- The halachic status of Judea, Samaria, and Gaza
- The building of Jerusalem
- The ingathering of exiles during the third period of redemption
- The love of Israel and senseless hatred
- Who is a Jew in the perspective of the generations
- The archaeological excavations in the City of David in the eyes of halacha.

In these essays, Rabbi Goren shows that there is no contemporary political or economic development that is, in his judgment, outside the scope and consideration of Jewish law

Another posthumously collected group of his writing is his *Torah HaMikra: Sermons on the Weekly Parsha in 5756*. In these writings, Rabbi Goren makes use of the *midrashic* sources and the great Biblical commentaries to read the text. The *divrei* Torah were given weekly at the Kommemiyut Avraham synagogue in Tel Aviv, which Rabbi Goren founded. His special contribution, according to Haim Fink, the editor of this work, was his capacity to express in a few brief words a great and exalted political or philosophical idea. These commentaries mainly involve a deep probing of one idea or question.

Another aspect of Rabbi Goren's mind and interests is revealed in his posthumously published, *Torat HaPhilosophia* (5758). In this work, Rabbi Goren examines the foundations of Jewish thought, including an inquiry into the question of whether an independent Jewish philosophy is possible at all. The work also contains a brief history of Jewish philosophical thought, giving special emphasis to the work of the Rambam. It also explores Greek thinking, Plato, and Aristotle in relation to Jewish thought. And it makes a profound effort at understanding central concepts in Jewish thought, such as Divine Providence.

Torat HaRefuah (5761) contains his writings on medical halacha. A great part of these are his answers to pressing questions of the day in medical ethics. The essays here reveal the thought behind the decisions that led to the halachic sanctioning of organ transplant, artificial insemination, and the establishment of skin banks in Israel. The volume contains essays on the following subjects:

- Responsibility of the Doctor Regarding the Life of the Patient
- Problems of Medical Experimentation done on the Critically Ill
- Boundary Lines between Life and Death according to Halacha
- Artificial Heart according to Halacha
- Liver Transplant according to Halacha
- Implanting an Egg from One Woman to Another

In these essays, once again, Rabbi Goren courageously tackled the most pressing medical questions of the day.

The most recent volume, *Terumat HaGoren*, contains halachic responsa on *Orach Chayim*.

Additional volumes of Rabbi Goren's responsa are in preparation.

There are those among Rabbi Goren's closest associates who suggest that had he not loved "action" so much, he might have written more. Certainly there are not forty volumes. The work on the *Yerushalmi* was never truly undertaken fully. Yet Rabbi Goren's literary legacy has its own unique weight and value, especially on certain subjects that he pioneered in its investigation. Most certainly the rulings on army life, the work in medical halacha, and the work done on the Temple Mount will continue to be referred to and cited for generations to come.

IN RETROSPECT: AFTERWORD

Chapter 73

Rabbi Goren's Relevance Today

One of the most commonplace, and yet sad, phenomena of human life is
how rapidly human glory fades from the world. It is only about a decade
since Rabbi Goren left the world and already there are signs of his memory
being marginalized. The yeshiva that he took such pride in founding near
the Kotel and *Har HaBayit*, the Idra Yeshiva, was closed. As Rabbi Goren
did not succeed in founding a political party in Israel, today there is no
stream of political thought that draws exclusively, or even primarily, from
his teachings. In this he is distinguished from his great teacher and
predecessor, Rabbi Avraham Yitzhak HaCohen Kook, and even from Rav
Kook's son, Rabbi Zvi Yehudah, who many in the settlement movement
today give their prime allegiance.

Rabbi Goren has no school of followers. Many of his colleagues,
including those who worked with him for many years in the military
rabbinate, are not strict followers of his way in teaching and in Torah. It
might be said that the reason for this is that the Torah of Rabbi Goren is
not taught in any single major philosophical work, but rather is scattered
throughout his writings, in his dozen or more books, and perhaps even
more importantly in his hundreds of responsa.

Once he was the sole *posek* in relation to halachic military
questions. Fortunately, competent successors have come, but this means
his rulings do not have the same inviolability they once had. Yet we see
today, time and time again, that when new and important halachic
questions are asked, Rabbi Goren's responsa are consulted.

The foundations he laid for the army rabbinate are also still in place. Generations of young soldiers have been able to go through the army, preserving and enhancing their religious identity, thanks to him. The prayers he composed are recited day after day, year after year by thousands who do not even know who wrote them.

His influence is also felt whenever there are controversial questions of medical halacha. In this area, too, the foundations he laid in ruling on certain kinds of questions, including organ transplant and artificial insemination, are fundamental to the subject.

Moreover, the kind of example and model he set, as a religious Jew in the army of Israel, has been followed by tens of thousands. In the early days, religious Jews had a relatively small role in the Israeli Army; with the years, they have entered all the elite units and taken greater responsibility for the physical defense of Israel. This is unfortunately not true for those like Rabbi Goren, who was himself at the highest level of learning. Also, there has been no spiritual leader comparable to him in stature who has since played a significant role in the Israeli Army.

It might also be said that his books, however rich in learning and deep in insight they are, have not become the curriculum of any institution, or the sine qua non for any field of learning. They give no sign of becoming required study in the *yeshivot*, even the *hesder yeshivot*. The large Hebrew trade publisher, *Yediot Ahronot*, maintains several of his books of Torah and holiday commentary in print.

Still, it is clear that many of the humane and insightful aspects of his halachic rulings (such as those permitting the second marriage of wives whose husbands were lost at sea) continue to stand at the heart of Jewish law.

Also it is clear that in certain areas of Jewish experience – for instance all that is connected with the Temple Mount and the restoration of Jewish prayer there – Rabbi Goren's work is seminal and essential. The distortion and demonization of his thought on these issues cannot detract from the persuasive power of learning and insight he reveals in his writing.

Whoever considers or decides on these issues in the future will be forced to take into account his thought on these questions.

Rabbi Goren's belief in the divine transmission of the Land of Israel to the Jewish people as sole possessors has hundreds of thousands of followers.

However, it is sadly true that this view, which Rabbi Goren regarded as the correct view for the people of Israel as a whole, is still the view of the minority of Israeli Jews. Furthermore, Rabbi Goren's concept of a unified Jewish people in the far more tribal and pluralistic Israel of today has diminished appeal.

In matters related to the Oslo process, Rabbi Goren's views have been vindicated. Much of the condemnation he received from the media of Israel toward the end of his days has proven mistaken. Yet the vindication of his views on this subject and of the understanding that the security of Israel must be fought for, still have not led to a revival of interest in his thought on these subjects. There are almost no biographical essays on the life of Rabbi Goren, and the intellectual interest – even from the National Religious camp – in his work has not been great. Needless to say, one major reason for this book is the hope of reviving that interest, and the hope that greater attention will be given to illuminating his life and thought.

Rabbi Goren's relevance to the kind of spiritual vision Israel continues to need should not be discounted. Against those who turn their backs on historical action and responsibility, Rabbi Goren argued about not relying on miracles in *Eretz Yisrael*. Miracles were for the time of wandering in the desert before entering the Land. The Jew, according to Rabbi Goren, once in the Land, must fight to make a place and maintain a place in the Land. The redemptive action of history is connected with this continual struggle, one that we should not expect to automatically end in our favor.

So too, Rabbi Goren's view of the world was repugnant to those who saw nothing in history but the senseless movement of incident and accident. Rabbi Goren saw the Jew's role in the Land of Israel as a redemptive one, requiring constant battle and struggle. He did not see an immediate and easy end to this.

His sense of the Jewish need for patience, strength, and faith in continuing the long struggle seems to speak more to our world in the early twenty-first century than it did at the time of the immediate wake of Oslo when Rabbi Goren left this world. Reality has sided with his vision of things, at least until now. He didn't just set an example, but a way of teaching that can guide many through the confusions of the present.

As a fighter, he had a view of the Jews returning to the Land as a warrior people, a people who, even against their will, must be prepared to struggle. Perhaps this vision in which the individual never stops testing himself, never stops making an effort, is the one that Israel most needs now.

The time has come for his great example to be an inspiration to the young in Israel, an inspiration to all those who would lead full lives in the service of God and Israel. Hopefully, more and more will be written about his life, greater and greater study devoted to his rulings, and his contribution to Israeli society more deeply and properly appreciated.

Chapter 74

LESSONS FOR TODAY

Rabbi Shlomo Goren's life story provides a set of teachings that, taken as a whole, provide a much-needed ethical guide to Israel today. Rabbi Goren's life was one of incredible devotion and dedication to the redemption of the people of Israel, to the building of the Jewish state, and to the service of God. He synthesized within himself and through his actions, qualities and values that today are considered exclusive possession of only one particular kind of Jew and Israeli. He was, on the one hand, a great student of Torah – one who from an early age showed tremendous brilliance – and throughout his life he continued to study, write, and teach, making a unique contribution to the whole world of Jewish learning. On the other hand, he was a man of action, whose physical courage in Israel's war for independence and recognition was legendary. For him, fighting for Israel was a primary moral duty, and his building of the foundations of the Israeli Army as a Jewish army is one of the great achievements of his life. He gave most of his study time to Torah, but he did not turn his back on the world of secular and university learning, and there, too, in his studies and teachings of philosophy he excelled. His hunger for knowledge was immense and as a *posek*, he delved into and mastered new fields of learning. Not only was he the first great modern *posek* connected with military life, but he was also a pioneer in all connected with medical ethics. As a *posek*, his compassion was immense, and his decisions that gave *agunot* from the loss of the Israeli ships *Eilat* and *Dakar* were models both of halachic scholarship and true social concern. Fierce in his love of justice, he was even determined in his concern for each and every Jew who he felt was suffering unjustly. Thus, in the notorious Langer case he drew upon himself the wrath of a great deal of the *old yishuv*'s religious establishment, but made certain that justice was done for two young people who had served the State of Israel.

Rabbi Goren believed in the creation of the Jewish state as historical manifestation of the Divine process of redemption. He pointed to the ingathering of the exiles and the Jewish winning of sovereignty in the Land of Israel as first signs, however incomplete, of the Messianic era to come. As one who lived through the time of the destruction of European Jewry, one who had lost many family members there, he believed most deeply in the Jewish state, as home and refuge, as the one true sanctuary for the Jewish people. Wherever he went throughout the world, he spoke with pride for Israel and was its defender in the deepest way.

At a time when so much of the discourse of Israeli life revolves around the needs and interests of particular sectors, ethnic groups, economic classes, political parties, etc., one central value of his stands out. All his life he struggled for the unity of the people of Israel, for a common cause and meaning. As the first chief army rabbi, he cancelled the separate religious units and strove to integrate soldiers of all kinds into a shared experience. He tried to teach others to think not of their own narrow interest, but of the well-being of the people as a whole. At the height of his greatest moments, even at the taking of the Temple Mount and the Kotel in 1967 in which he played such an important inspirational role, he turned to the needs of individual soldiers and their families.

His belief in the Jewish people and their story, in their covenant with God, and their historic and eternal connection with the Land of Israel can give us new strength at a time when so many are filled with confusion and doubt. The struggles he went through were immense, as have been the struggles the Jewish people have gone through. But with faith like his, with vision and inspiration, with his heart in the love of God and Israel, enemies may be overcome and the future can be one of blessing and redemption.

SELECTED BIBLIOGRAPHY

Books with sections about Rabbi Goren

Alfassi, Dr. Yitzhak, ed. *HaMa'alot L'Shlomo: A Memorial Book in Halacha and Aggada to Maran HaGaon HaAdir Sar HaTorah HaRav Shlomo Goren.*

Published on his first *yahrtzeit*, 24 *MarCheshvan* 5756. This memorial work contains two fine biographical sketches and important articles on various aspects of Rabbi Goren's work, as well as articles by Rabbi Goren himself.

Michelson, Menachem. *Tzahal b'Chaylo Israeli Army Encyclopedia*, Volume 16, Section on the Military Rabbinate, pp. 81–128, Revivim Sifrut Maariv, 1982.

This excellent account of the development of the army rabbinate contains much valuable information on Rabbi Goren's life that appears in no other source.

Ehrlich, Israel. *People and Events in the History of Israel.* Tel Aviv: Morasha Publishers, 5754. Chapter 13, "The Voice of the Shofar on the Temple Mount," pp. 190–226.

An outstanding and inspirational chapter of this work is devoted to the life of Rabbi Goren, and especially connected with the events of the Six Day War.

A selection of books in print by Rabbi Goren

Meishiv Milchama, HaIdra Rabba.

Responsa on army-related questions (Volumes 1–3).

Har HaBayit (volume 4 of *Meishiv Milchama*), HaIdra Rabba, *Yediot Ahronot*, 5752.

This presents comprehensive halachic and historical research on *Har HaMoriah* including up-to-date maps.

Torat HaMedina, HaIdra Rabba, Mesorah La'am, 5756.

This is a halachic historical research on subjects that are in the center of Israeli public life since its founding.

Torat HaMikra: Sermons on Parshat HaShavua, HaIdra Rabba, 5756.

Moadei Yisrael, HaIdra Rabba, Mesorah La'am, 5757.

Research and revelation of new contents on the subject of the holidays of Israel.

Torat HaPhilosophia, HaIdra Rabba, 5758.

A collection of essays on Jewish philosophy.

Mishna HaMedina, HaIdra Rabba, 5759.

A halachic historical research on subjects that are at the center of Israeli public life since the founding of the state.

Torah HaRefua: Halachic Research on Questions of Medical Ethics. HaIdra Rabba, 5761.

Terumat HaGoren: Halachic Responsa on Orach Chayim, Part One, HaIdra Rabba, 5764.

Books on related subjects

Shragai, Nadiv. *The Temple Mount Conflict*. Keter, 1995.
Narkiss, Uzi. *Soldier of Jerusalem*. Valentine Mitchell, 1998.
Narkiss, Uzi. *The Liberation of Jerusalem*. Valentine Mitchell, 1983.

Selected articles

Cohen, HaRav Shear Yashuv, *"Gaon HaTorah HaAm v'Ha'aretz from HaMa'alot l'Shlomo,"* pp. 20–45.

This is the finest appreciation of Rabbi Goren's scholarship that has as yet been written.

Alfassi, HaRav Dr. Yitzhak, *"Kavim leToldeto Rabbeinu HaGadol, ztz"l,"* from *HaMa'alot l'Shlomo*, pp. 15–19.

The best concise summary of Rabbi Goren's life written by one of his most devoted and learned followers.

Cohen, Yoel, "The Political Role of the Israeli Chief Rabbinate in the Temple Mount Question," Jewish Political Studies Review, Volume 11–12, Spring 1999.

Newspaper articles

Arad, Aryeh. "Portrait of the Chief Rabbi as Country Child," *Ha'aretz*, October 18, 1972.

Bashan, Rafael. "In Tel Aviv as in *Tzahal:* I Will go Always in the Path of Beit Hillel," *Yediot Ahronot*, June 18, 1971.

Court, Andy. "Mounting Battle over Agam Monument," *Jerusalem Post*, May 16, 1987.

Goldberg, Abraham. "Israel Prize Winner," *Jerusalem Post*, August 15, 1962.

Goren, Shlomo. "Battle for the Soul of Eastern European Jewry," *Jerusalem Post*.

——. "A Jewish Peace Plan," *Jerusalem Post*, March 4, 1988.

——. "Certificates of Conversion: Valid for Israel Only," *Jerusalem Post*, March 3, 1989.

——. "Do Torah Scholars Enhance Peace?" *Jerusalem Post*, June 14, 1990.

——. "Halacha and the People's Will," November 25, 1988.

——. "Israel Needs its Religion," *Jerusalem Post,* February 13, 1987.

——. "No Fear of God or State," *Jerusalem Post*, January 2, 1987.

——. "The Duty to the Patient," *Jerusalem Post*, February 12, 1988

——. "The Holy Land and the Value of Life," *Jerusalem* Post, October 6, 1989.

——. "The Hasmoneans' Menorah," *Jerusalem Post, D*ecember 9, 1988.

——. "The Prophetic Vision," *Jerusalem Post*, April 20, 1988.

——. "When the Jews Failed Eretz Yisrael," *Jerusalem Post*, September 20, 1988.

Huberman, Haggai. "Twenty-five Years to the Liberation of Jerusalem," *HaTzofeh*, May 29, 1992.

Katzman, Avi. "Goren Purified *Mamzerim*, Permitted *Agunot* to Remarry, and Enabled Autopsies," *Ha'aretz*, October 30, 1994.

Nakdimon, Shlomo. "Four Days in Poland," *Yediot Ahronot*, May 25, 1984

——. "Surrender of Hebron," *Yediot Ahronot*, April 18, 1972.

——. "The I Accuse of Chief Rabbi Goren in the Affair of the 'Brother and Sister'," *Yediot Ahronot*, January 5, 1973.

Shavit, Yosef. "HaRav Goren: I will fight against all scientific work that violates Torah," *Yediot Ahronot*, August 8, 1981.

Wallfish, Asher. "Blowing His Own Trumpet," *Jerusalem Post*, August 28, 1981.

About the Author

Shalom Freedman is the author of seven previous books on Jewish subjects, the most recent of which is *Small Acts of Kindness: Striving for Derech Eretz in Everyday Life* (Urim).